"A book on Ecclesiastes might seem strange ⌐⌐⌐ many books there is no end; and much study is a weariness of the flesh, but the rich truths present in this book are imperative to our full formation as the people of God. The writers have wrung Jesus out of this book, and whether you are planning on preaching a series on Ecclesiastes or just using this to study the Word of God, your heart will be stirred and your mind informed."

Matt Chandler, lead pastor, The Village Church

"The book of Ecclesiastes is God's powerful reminder of the emptiness in life when devoid of Himself. However, Danny and Jon open our eyes to the beauty of life's meaning once lived in obedience to God. I wish there were another chapter, it's so refreshing!"

Johnny Hunt, senior pastor, First Baptist Church, Woodstock, Georgia

"Nothing is more refreshing than when a book delivers what the cover promises. *Exalting Jesus in Ecclesiastes* does just that and more. This book not only exalts Jesus, but it extracts truth in a compelling way with a perfect blend of solid exegesis, relevant exposition, and personal exhortation. Any preacher or teacher wanting to study a book on wisdom written by the wisest man who ever lived (outside of Jesus, of course!) would be wise to have this one right by his side."

James Merritt, lead pastor, Cross Pointe Church, Duluth, Georgia

CHRIST-CENTERED
Exposition

AUTHORS **Daniel L. Akin and Jonathan Akin**
SERIES EDITORS **David Platt, Daniel L. Akin, and Tony Merida**

CHRIST-CENTERED

Exposition

EXALTING JESUS IN

ECCLESIASTES

HOLMAN
REFERENCE

NASHVILLE, TENNESSEE

Christ-Centered Exposition Commentary: Exalting Jesus in Ecclesiastes

© Copyright 2016 by Daniel L. Akin and Jon Akin

B&H Publishing Group
Nashville, Tennessee

All rights reserved.

ISBN 978-0-8054-9776-2

Dewey Decimal Classification: 220.7

Subject Heading: BIBLE. O.T. ECCLESIASTES—COMMENTARIES\JESUS
CHRIST

Unless otherwise stated all Scripture quotations are from the *Holman
Christian Standard Bible*® Copyright 1999, 2000, 2002, 2003, 2009 by
Holman Bible Publishers. Used by permission.

Scripture quotations marked ESV are from The Holy Bible, English
Standard Version, copyright © 2001 by Crossway Bibles, a division of Good
News Publishers. Used by permission. All rights reserved.

Scripture quotations marked NIV 1984 are from the Holy Bible, New
International Version, copyright © 1973, 1978, 1984 by International Bible
Society. Used by permission. All rights reserved worldwide.

Scripture quotations marked NKJV is taken from the New King James
Version®. Copyright © 1982 by Thomas Nelson. Used by permission.
All rights reserved.

Printed in the United States of America
5 6 7 8 9 10 • 25 24 23 22 21
VP

SERIES DEDICATION

Dedicated to Adrian Rogers and John Piper. They have taught us to love the gospel of Jesus Christ, to preach the Bible as the inerrant Word of God, to pastor the church for which our Savior died, and to have a passion to see all nations gladly worship the Lamb.

—David Platt, Tony Merida, and Danny Akin
March 2013

AUTHORS' DEDICATION

To Ashley and Charlotte, our wives, whom we love
and with whom we enjoy life

"Enjoy life with the wife you love all the days
of your fleeting life." (Eccl 9:9)

TABLE OF CONTENTS

ACKNOWLEDGMENTS

Ecclesiastes 4:9-12 details the goodness of God in the relationships He has given us. Two are certainly better than one! There are so many people who have been a blessing in our lives and made an impact on this project. We are thankful to faithful scholars and expositors who greatly aided our exposition of Ecclesiastes. We are grateful for men like Alistair Begg, Matt Chandler, Duane Garrett, Johnny Hunt, and Tim Keller.

And I (Jon) am grateful to God to be able to partner on this project with my dad, who has faithfully taught me the Scriptures my entire life. This whole project has been a great blessing to me!

Furthermore, we are grateful to God for our families and children and grandchildren. They truly make obeying the command of Ecclesiastes to enjoy every one of God's gifts very, very easy.

Finally, we are eternally grateful for Jesus, who is the point of Ecclesiastes. We pray that God would use this project to make people wise for salvation through faith in Jesus Christ (2 Tim 3:15).

SERIES INTRODUCTION

Augustine said, "Where Scripture speaks, God speaks." The editors of the Christ-Centered Exposition Commentary series believe that where God speaks, the pastor must speak. God speaks through His written Word. We must speak from that Word. We believe the Bible is God breathed, authoritative, inerrant, sufficient, understandable, necessary, and timeless. We also affirm that the Bible is a Christ-centered book; that is, it contains a unified story of redemptive history of which Jesus is the hero. Because of this Christ-centered trajectory that runs from Genesis 1 through Revelation 22, we believe the Bible has a corresponding global-missions thrust. From beginning to end, we see God's mission as one of making worshipers of Christ from every tribe and tongue worked out through this redemptive drama in Scripture. To that end we must preach the Word.

In addition to these distinct convictions, the Christ-Centered Exposition Commentary series has some distinguishing characteristics. First, this series seeks to display exegetical accuracy. What the Bible says is what we want to say. While not every volume in the series will be a verse-by-verse commentary, we nevertheless desire to handle the text carefully and explain it rightly. Those who teach and preach bear the heavy responsibility of saying what God has said in His Word and declaring what God has done in Christ. We desire to handle God's Word faithfully, knowing that we must give an account for how we have fulfilled this holy calling (Jas 3:1).

Second, the Christ-Centered Exposition Commentary series has pastors in view. While we hope others will read this series, such as parents, teachers, small-group leaders, and student ministers, we desire to provide a commentary busy pastors will use for weekly preparation of biblically faithful and gospel-saturated sermons. This series is not academic in nature. Our aim is to present a readable and pastoral style of commentaries. We believe this aim will serve the church of the Lord Jesus Christ.

Third, we want the Christ-Centered Exposition Commentary series to be known for the inclusion of helpful illustrations and theologically driven applications. Many commentaries offer no help in illustrations, and few offer any kind of help in application. Often those that do offer illustrative material and application unfortunately give little serious attention to the text. While giving ourselves primarily to explanation, we also hope to serve readers by providing inspiring and illuminating illustrations coupled with timely and timeless application.

Finally, as the name suggests, the editors seek to exalt Jesus from every book of the Bible. In saying this, we are not commending wild allegory or fanciful typology. We certainly believe we must be constrained to the meaning intended by the divine Author Himself, the Holy Spirit of God. However, we also believe the Bible has a messianic focus, and our hope is that the individual authors will exalt Christ from particular texts. Luke 24:25-27,44-47 and John 5:39,46 inform both our hermeneutics and our homiletics. Not every author will do this the same way or have the same degree of Christ-centered emphasis. That is fine with us. We believe faithful exposition that is Christ centered is not monolithic. We do believe, however, that we must read the whole Bible as Christian Scripture. Therefore, our aim is both to honor the historical particularity of each biblical passage and to highlight its intrinsic connection to the Redeemer.

The editors are indebted to the contributors of each volume. The reader will detect a unique style from each writer, and we celebrate these unique gifts and traits. While distinctive in their approaches, the authors share a common characteristic in that they are pastoral theologians. They love the church, and they regularly preach and teach God's Word to God's people. Further, many of these contributors are younger voices. We think these new, fresh voices can serve the church well, especially among a rising generation that has the task of proclaiming the Word of Christ and the Christ of the Word to the lost world.

We hope and pray this series will serve the body of Christ well in these ways until our Savior returns in glory. If it does, we will have succeeded in our assignment.

David Platt
Daniel L. Akin
Tony Merida
Series Editors
February 2013

Ecclesiastes

Everything Is Meaningless without Jesus
ECCLESIASTES 1:1-18 AND 12:8-14

Main Idea: Everything is meaningless without Jesus.

I. Everything Is Meaningless Because All of Our Activity Is Pointless (1:3-11).

II. Everything Is Meaningless Because Nothing Satisfies (1:12-18).

III. Everything Is Meaningless Because Our Frustration Is Meant to Drive Us to Christ (12:8-14).

Bill Murray plays the main character, weatherman Phil Connors, in the comedy *Groundhog Day* (1993). His character relives February second—Groundhog Day—over and over again in Punxsutawney, Pennsylvania, where the main festival takes place. Some obsessive viewers speculate Phil might have relived the same day for three decades. What does Phil do to cope with this monotonous prison? What does he do to try to find meaning when it seems like nothing he does really matters from one day to the next? He looks for happiness in different experiences. He tries all kinds of things in his quest for some semblance of meaning.

Phil turns to hedonistic pleasures and denies himself nothing. If it feels good, he does it! There's one scene in the diner where he gorges himself on a table full of food, drinking coffee straight from the pot and smoking a cigarette. He punches out a guy who really annoys him. He seduces women into bed with him. When that fails to satisfy, Phil turns to greed. He robs an armored car and uses the money to buy the car and the clothes he has always wanted. He tries to live out the life he could not before. Next, Phil turns to despair. Faced with the reality that he cannot escape from this curse, Phil takes his life multiple times, but he wakes up again every time right back in Punxsutawney. Finally, Phil turns to knowledge. He tries to learn and better himself. He takes up piano, ice sculpting, French poetry, and more to become an educated, well-rounded man.

Phil does not wake up on February third until he finally reaches contentment in his current circumstance. Only then is the curse lifted.

The last time he relives February second he looks into the eyes of a woman he has fallen in love with, Rita, and he says, "I don't know what will happen tomorrow; all I know is I'm happy right now." That's kind of the point of the book of Ecclesiastes. We are stuck in a monotonous prison where nothing we do really changes anything, and the only way to live a meaningful life in this meaningless existence is to find satisfaction and contentment in what God has given us.

There is a really interesting scene in the movie, early on in Phil's experience, when he is trying to figure out what is going on. He sits at a bar in a bowling alley with two local guys who are drunk, and he asks them this question: "What would you do if you were stuck in one place, and every day was the same, and nothing you did really mattered?"

One of the men stares into his beer mug and says, "Yep, that about sums it up for me."

As Matt Chandler said, "Life is more like *Groundhog Day* than we want to admit," and to prove the point, Chandler walks through a person's typical day asking, "What will you do on Monday?" (Chandler, "Sixth Sense"). Your alarm will go off at 6:00 a.m., you will hit the snooze to sleep ten more minutes, and then you will stumble into the bathroom to brush your teeth and shower. You will get dressed, jump in your car, sit in traffic, and then finally get to work at your business or classroom or factory. You will work for a few hours and then take a break to eat lunch. Then you will get back to work for a few more hours, punch out, maybe hit the gym on the way home, and then eat dinner. You will sit on the couch and watch TV for a little bit, and then you will hop in bed. Guess what you will do Tuesday?!

We are stuck in a rut going through the motions trying to figure out what all of this means. There is a monotonous drudgery to life. Supervisors understand this reality, so they try to break the monotony with Hawaiian-shirt days or casual Fridays. And people deal with this reality in many different ways. I remember one of my college professors describing a factory job that he worked in college to pay tuition. He was surrounded by men in their 40s and 50s who had worked the same job in this factory for decades, standing on the assembly line doing the same thing hour after hour, day after day, week after week, month after month, year after year, and decade after decade. He said the men would talk all week about how they could not wait to punch out on Friday so they could go to the bar, get smashed, stay drunk all weekend, sober up by Monday morning, and get back to work. The only way they knew to cope with the redundancy and boredom of their lives was to distract themselves for a short while, so they lived week to week for the escape.

Some people look to substances; others look to pleasurable experiences; others pour themselves into their jobs, hoping success will make their lives meaningful; others turn to romantic relationships or accumulating possessions. Some even look to religion, hoping these rituals will give their life a semblance of meaning or transcendence or purpose.

In Ecclesiastes we find a guy faced with the monotony of life who tried to find meaning in all of those things and more, and in the end he concludes that everything is meaningless. Ecclesiastes was written by the "Teacher" or "Preacher." The Hebrew word denotes the leader of a congregation—a Pastor (Eswine, *Recovering Eden*, 3). Who is he? He is the "Son of David, king in Jerusalem" (1:1). Solomon is the only candidate because he is the only one of David's sons who ruled over a united Israel from Jerusalem (see Eccl 1:12; 1 Chr 29:25). Plus, Solomon's life experience matches the experience of the author. Solomon's responsibility for this work should not be surprising.[1] When David died, he handed the kingdom of Israel over to his son Solomon. God came to Solomon in a dream and told him that anything he asked of God would be granted to him. Solomon was young and inexperienced, so he asked for wisdom in order to have the ability to rule the nation well and uphold justice (1 Kgs 3:5-15). God granted Solomon's request, and Solomon used his great wisdom to rule the kingdom. One of the ways Solomon established a glorious kingdom was through his thousands of wise sayings and songs that people from all over the world came to hear (1 Kgs 4:29-34). Much of his wisdom is now contained in Proverbs, Song of Solomon, and Ecclesiastes.

However, the wisest man in the ancient world became a greedy, lustful, power-hungry, idolatrous fool. He violated the kingly commands of Deuteronomy 17 and accumulated possessions as well as women for himself. He had seven hundred wives and three hundred concubines (1 Kgs 11:3). The foreign women he married pulled his heart away from Yahweh to false gods (1 Kgs 11:1-8). He did not deny himself anything he wanted. As a result he ruined his kingdom, and God told Solomon that following his death his kingdom would be divided during his son's reign (1 Kgs 11:9-13).

---

[1] For a good discussion of Solomonic authorship, read Jim Hamilton, *God's Glory in Salvation through Judgment* (Wheaton: Crossway, 2010), 314–15.

Tradition says that Ecclesiastes reveals an older, repentant Solomon contemplating his mistakes and what he has learned. Johnny Hunt says Ecclesiastes appears to be the kind of book a person would write near the close of life, reflecting on life's experiences and the lessons learned (Hunt, *Ecclesiastes*, 2). We have no way of verifying whether this is the case, but the book at least seems to take on that tone. And in the conclusion the father warns his son not to follow in his footsteps (12:12). Solomon's message in Ecclesiastes is just as relevant today. People think to themselves all the time, *If I could just have more money, more pleasure, or more success, then I would really be happy*. Solomon had everything and tried everything, and in Ecclesiastes, perhaps at the end of his life, he tells us, "No! All of that is meaningless."

Ecclesiastes 1:2 gives the main point of the book when it states that everything in human existence is "*hevel* of *hevels*." To say that life is as meaningless as it could possibly be, it uses the Hebrew superlative form. For example, the "holy of holies" is the most holy place on the planet. The "Song of Songs" is the greatest song Solomon ever wrote. Thus, *hevel* of *hevels* means "as meaningless as possible." The word is used more than 30 times in the book, and it literally means "breath" or "vapor." The *vapor* connotation carries the idea of *fleeting*. When you breathe on a cold day, you can see your breath for a moment, and then it vanishes. James gets at a similar idea when he says life is mist that vanishes tomorrow (Jas 4:14). Metaphorically the word *hevel* is used over and over again in Ecclesiastes to express the idea that life is vain or meaningless or futile or absurd. So basically the word carries the concept that life is meaningless, pointless, worthless, or frustrating because it is frail and fleeting. It can carry all of these connotations, and context really must determine which specific nuance of the word the interpreter chooses (see Garrett, *Proverbs, Ecclesiastes, Song of Songs*, 282–83).

Often in the Bible, the word is used in connection with idols (Jer 16:19; Zech 10:2), and that is something of the meaning here in Ecclesiastes. People try to find satisfaction in created things rather than the Creator, and seeking satisfaction in anything or anyone other than God is idolatry. The search does not work because created things cannot bring ultimate satisfaction. It's not that pleasure, money, stuff, sex, or success are bad things in and of themselves, but when they become ultimate things to us, they let us down. You see, a *good thing* turned into a *God thing* becomes a *bad thing*. It becomes an idol. We will see throughout this book that success, possessions, pleasure, and even religion are ultimately meaningless. They look like they can bring us true happiness, but it is a mirage. The problem is that none of these things is ever enough, and they do not last. Again, *hevel* carries the idea of fleeting and meaningless. Whatever you try to build your life on other than Jesus is ultimately utterly meaningless.

The garden of Eden, which God created for Adam and Eve, was "very good" (Gen 1:31)—a fruitful and meaningful place to live. But when Adam and Eve rebelled against God, they were expelled from the garden, and a guard was placed at the gateway on the east side (Gen 3:24). Ecclesiastes drives home the point that life in this fallen world east of Eden is futile and meaningless.

A parallel from Paul in the New Testament illumines this backdrop. While Ecclesiastes is never directly quoted in the New Testament, Romans 8:20 seems to be an allusion. Paul uses the same word (*mataiotēs*) that the Septuagint uses in Ecclesiastes 1:2 when he talks about the curse God imposed on creation because of human sin. Romans 8:20-21 says,

> *For the creation was subjected to* futility—*not willingly, but because of Him who subjected it—in the hope that the creation itself will also be set free from the bondage of corruption into the glorious freedom of God's children.* (emphasis added)

When man rebelled against God's design (Gen 3), a frustrating curse was brought into the world. Now nothing works right, and we live in a broken world where we suffer the consequences of going our own way. Disease, death, poverty, evil, injustice, and more characterize our current existence. Therefore, according to Paul, the fallen creation is futile and in bondage, screaming for rescue.

The creation of humanity and the fall into sin are the background to Solomon's observations of life in this broken world. God created the world good with a design for everything. God created the world as a perfect home for His children—humanity—and gave good gifts like food, drink, relationships, and sex. God designed these gifts to be used as He intended and not as ends in and of themselves. They were designed to cause our hearts to worship our Creator. So when we eat, drink, or enjoy sex with our spouse, these activities are intended to elicit a reaction of praise and gratitude to God for His good gifts.

Instead, we rebelled against God's good design and began using His gifts in ways He did not intend. We turned them into ends rather than means. We sought to find satisfaction in the created things rather than the Creator God, and that brought a curse on the world (Rom 1:18-32). Now there are death and brokenness, and things do not work right. We abuse the gifts so that now food becomes gluttony, drink become drunkenness, and sex becomes adultery. We reject our God-given roles in marriage. Labor to provide for our families is now frustrating and difficult. Genesis 3 says sweat and frustrating fruit production will characterize our work. And we will ultimately return to the dust from which we were created (Gen 3:8-19). Thus Ecclesiastes describes the meaninglessness and frustration of life in a Genesis 3 world.

The atheist philosopher Bertrand Russell captures well the realities of the world people find themselves in as described by the preacher of Ecclesiastes. He writes,

> We stand on the shore of an ocean, crying to the night and the emptiness; sometimes a voice answers out of the darkness. But it is a voice of one drowning; and in a moment the silence returns. The world seems to me quite dreadful; the unhappiness of most people is very great, and I often wonder how they all endure it. To know people well is to know their tragedy: it is usually the central thing about which their lives are built. And I suppose if they did not live most of the time in the things of the moment, they would not be able to go on. (Russell, *Autobiography*, 1,994)

Like children who do not say thank you for Christmas presents, we now worship the gifts rather than the Giver. We look to temporary things like pleasure, sex, money, stuff, popularity, and success for lasting satisfaction they cannot give. Remember, it's not that these things are bad. They are good gifts from God. But when we turn a gift into a god from which we seek ultimate satisfaction, it will let us down and enslave us. East of Eden and separated from God, we live in a cursed, meaningless existence seeking lasting joy in things that eventually let us down! This is the reality of life "under the sun" that Solomon unfolds for us in this book.

Everything Is Meaningless Because All of Our Activity Is Pointless
ECCLESIASTES 1:3-11

Solomon begins by asking a question to prove his main point that everything is meaningless. He asks in 1:3, "What does a man gain for all his efforts [ESV, "toil"] that he labors at under the sun?" The Hebrew word translated *gain* is unique to Ecclesiastes, and it means "profit or advantage" (Kidner, *Ecclesiastes*, 24). *Effort/labor*, another key idea in the book, recalls similar language from the curse of Genesis 3, where God said labor would be painful (Gen 3:17-19). And *under the sun* is an important phrase found about 30 times in the book. It means Solomon is looking at the question of meaning from an earthly perspective. If this world is all there is—if there is no God, no afterlife, and no final judgment—then everything is meaningless. The phrase does not necessitate an atheist outlook but rather an uncertainty about what lies beyond this life, its experiences and observations. Solomon expects a negative answer to his question about profit under the sun. If this life is all there is, then what is the point of our existence since all of our activity does not bring a net gain? All of our work, education, and love really gain us nothing because nothing really ever changes. W. A. Criswell said it well: "You look at time and tide and history, and it brings you to infinite despair" ("The Pattern of Pessimism").

I was a nerd in middle school, but I thought I was so cool because I rocked a "No Fear" T-shirt up and down the hallways. I had this light-blue "No Fear" shirt that said, "He who dies with the most toys still dies. No Fear!" I thought the shirt was so awesome because I was wearing it in the face of the goofy bumper-sticker notion that the person who dies with the most toys wins at life. Solomon's point is similar to that "No Fear" shirt. You do not get to take the fruits of your labor and activity beyond the grave if this life is all there is. Thus, there is no real profit to our activity.

Jesus asks a similar question in Mark 8:36: "What does it profit a man if he gains the whole world and yet loses his soul?" The answer is, "Nothing!" How much you make, how much you learn, and how popular you are is meaningless because life without God is futile (Hunt, *Ecclesiastes*, 3). As Tim Keller points out, the author of Ecclesiastes is pushing us to the logical conclusion of our position, exposing any philosophy that would seek to live life without God as the ultimate foundation. If this life is all there is, then what permanent value is your life? Keller explains that we ask the question, What's in it for me? in the small things, but we do not seem to ask it over the whole of our life. If I told you to show up in the parking lot tomorrow morning at 9:00 a.m., you would ask "Why?" If I said, "Just show up," then you would reply, "What's in it for me? Why should I come? What will I be doing?" And yet, we do

not ask those questions of our lives. What's the overall profit to what I am doing (Keller, "Problem of Meaning")?)
The author's point is that if this life is all there is, then there is no profit to your life. The poem in Ecclesiastes 1:4-11 points to repetitive cycles in nature to prove the point that nothing is gained from all our activity. Like a good sage Solomon observes nature in order to extrapolate wisdom for our lives. The natural cycles demonstrate that all our activity is pointless because nothing changes despite a whole lot of activity. The poem paints the picture that we are trapped in a monotonous prison (Garrett, *Ecclesiastes*, 284).

Ecclesiastes 1:4 points to the cycle of generations while the earth stays the same. Ecclesiastes will repeatedly paint the portrait of life in a Genesis 5 world where death reigns and nothing changes. As Jerome said,("What's more vain than this vanity: that the earth, which was made for humans stays—but humans themselves, the lords of the earth suddenly dissolve into the dust" (cited in Longman, *Ecclesiastes*, 67). This is the absurd reality: humanity dies and a new generation comes, but the earth stays the same.)

Solomon gives three examples from nature and three examples where human experience mirrors the natural cycles (1:5-8). He compares the sun to an exhausted track runner who runs lap after lap, looks like he is moving somewhere, but is actually just going in circles (1:5) (Garrett, *Ecclesiastes*, 285). The wind also gusts in circles (1:6). There is lots of activity, but nothing changes. The east-to-west observation of verse 5 and the north-to-south observation of verse 6 make up a merism that pictures the totality of the world (Murphy, *Proverbs, Ecclesiastes, Song of Songs*, 180). The whole of nature is characterized by monotony. The last cycle is that of the oceans (1:7). All of the streams of the earth run into the sea but the water level stays the same. There is no net gain!

The task is never done; it just repeats itself again and again. There is no satisfaction under the sun. The universe is trapped in a meaningless cycle that never ultimately accomplishes anything, and human experience as a whole mirrors this. Our existence can be characterized as one of monotony and pointlessness. It is the same old, same old. We all feel this frustration from time to time, do we not? You walk into the kitchen and the sink is full of dishes, so you roll up your sleeves, clean them, and put them away. You walk back into the kitchen the next morning, and what is there? Dishes! The laundry basket is overflowing with clothes, so you throw them in the washing machine, then the dryer, and then you fold them and put them away. You walk into your closet and what do you see? Clothes piled high in the laundry basket. These are the facts of life: more bills, more e-mails, more haircuts, more grass to mow, and it never ends. People try their own ways of "breaking free" from this monotony, as Kelly Clarkson sings about in "Breakaway" and Reba McEntire in "Is There Life Out There?" People have midlife crises, affairs, and career shifts trying to break free from the dissatisfaction in their lives. Swindoll is right: such people are simply "chasing the wind" (*Living on the Ragged Edge*, 25). Even Christians try to deal with this and often not in helpful ways. I remember listening to a preacher talk about these realities, and he called people away from the dissatisfaction of their lives to try something new. While it was not his intent, I remember walking away from that sermon thinking to myself that people walked into this room dissatisfied with their spouse and now think they may need to find someone else, or dissatisfied with their job and are now thinking of quitting under the faulty notion that they will easily find a "job they love." But like the sea you are never full, it is never enough, and you are never satisfied. You move on to another relationship, and the same dissatisfaction persists because you never dealt with the lack of contentment you had before. You just rearranged the pieces. You are at your new job and just as bored as you were before. The grass is always greener, and you could always get more money, another partner, a bigger promotion, a nicer house; but just as the sea is never full, it will never be enough for you!

Therefore, Solomon concludes in verse 8 that our existence is full of weariness. He gives three behaviors to parallel the sun, wind, and sea. He contends that we cannot say enough, see enough, or hear enough. We cannot say enough words to find meaning in the midst of this monotony. The eye will never be able to see it all. There are always more sights to see, experiences to take in, and pictures to look at. For some there is always one more pornographic image to try to find pleasure in because the experience does not last. And the ear has never heard it all. There is always more gossip to spread, songs to hear, jokes to listen to, or flirtatious words to enjoy. Nothing we can say, see, or hear can bring meaning to this redundancy.

As the Rolling Stones song says, no matter how much we try, we "can't get no satisfaction." Our desires are never satiated. We are not happy, nor are we content. We always want more. We think if we could just get two floors up in this building, or if we could just get the bigger house in the gated neighborhood, or if we had more gadgets, then we will have arrived (Begg, "Word to the Wise"). We keep waiting for a change in circumstances that will make us happy, and honestly we live our entire lives like that. You are frustrated under the lack of freedom in your parent's house as a child and think to yourself, *I cannot wait till I get my license and go to college because then I will be free and happy.* Then you get into college and think, *I cannot wait till I get out of all this boring studying and start doing a job that I really love.* Then you graduate and take the job and say to yourself, *If only I could find someone to love and get married, then I would be happy.* Then you find someone, fall in love, get married, and think, *If we could just have a family, then life would be complete.* So you have kids and then think, *If I could get promoted so I could make more money to provide for my family, then* . . . The cycle never ends. You keeping thinking, *If I can just get "there," everything will be different,* but when you get there nothing is different.

The author makes this point clear in verses 9-11. There is nothing new under the sun; nothing ever changes. People object to that truth; they are wrong. Technological advances, for example, do not discount Solomon's contention. As Begg points out, yes, we put a man on the moon, but there was nothing for him to do there except stare at the earth ("Word to the Wise"). The fundamental events of life remain the same: birth, marriage, family, work, and death (Garrett, *Ecclesiastes,* 288). We use the phrase "nothing new under the sun" in our own parlance, and we do not use it as a pronouncement on inventions but rather to say, "The more things change, the more they stay the same" (Kidner, *Ecclesiastes,* 26). The human race is the same bunch of sinners it has always been, and nothing we have done really makes a difference.

Solomon says that no one will ultimately be remembered. Again, someone might object that we remember some figures from the past, but the vast billions who have lived on planet Earth never gain lasting renown. Most live and die unremembered. We do not remember our great, great-grandparents. Nothing really changes for anyone. You punch in and punch out over and over till you punch out for the last time. And when you retire, your company will throw a party, give you a gift with a plaque, and the next day someone else will replace you. The sun will rise, the business will go on, and eventually you will be forgotten. The business will carry on without you. Those are the facts of life under the sun. It's all meaningless and frustrating. What value is your life?

People try to find meaning in an individual's life at their funeral by saying, "She made the world a better place" (Keller, "Problem of Meaning"). But the Teacher says, "Nonsense." You did not really change anything. That's why *Les Miserables* raises questions such as: Will you be remembered when you die? Do your life and death really have any meaning? Could it be that your life is one big lie? Despite the claims of Jay Z and Fall Out Boys that they will be remembered for centuries, they will not! We are here for a few decades; then we are all forgotten. Death is the great equalizer, and that is the ultimate absurdity. We all step on the treadmill of life and try to outrun death with all of our activity but to no avail. The Grim Reaper is faster than all of us. He catches us all. All of our "new" innovations have only allowed us to postpone death for a little while longer. So, faced with this bleak reality, Solomon searches for meaning and satisfaction, but . . .

Everything Is Meaningless Because Nothing Satisfies
ECCLESIASTES 1:12-18

Solomon moves from what he has observed in nature to what we can learn from his experiences (1:12–2:26). He gives personal testimony that he tried everything and nothing satisfied. Everything was meaningless. He says, "I, the Teacher, have been king over Israel in Jerusalem" (1:12), which seems to indicate that he is older now with life experience. He goes on a wisdom search of the world, and he concludes that it is a miserable task that God gave to "Adam's sons."[2] This language recalls the imposed curse of Genesis 3 where toil becomes burdensome and our activities in the world are under this curse (cf. Rom 8:18-21).

All of our activity is like chasing the wind. Our girls love blowing bubbles outside on a warm day. Like all kids, they run around trying to catch the bubbles and the moment they touch them the bubbles disappear in their hand. That is the idea here. Our efforts in this fallen world are like trying to catch the wind in our hand. What would we do if we went outside and found a man with a net in the parking lot trying to catch wind? Call for a psych evaluation? Yet all of our exertion to find meaning and satisfaction in things like pleasure, possessions, money, or success are just that crazy. Sure, they look like worthwhile pursuits, but

---

[2] This is the literal translation of the Hebrew phrase translated "people" in the HCSB.

Solomon exposes them. They are grasping at the air. Solomon says that it does not matter where or in what you try to find meaning, you will fail. He has seen and done it all, and he came back empty. As with Psalm 73, the author is teetering on the edge of skepticism. Faith does not seem to be working like it should. A few years ago I met regularly with a guy I was mentoring. He and his wife were struggling with infertility. One day we met early at McDonald's, and he came in very upset. He told me that a guy at his work came into the factory cussing the previous day because he had accidentally gotten his girlfriend pregnant. My friend was distraught because he and his wife had begged God for a child, and here was a guy who did not even want a child but was going to become a dad. Many of us face this kind of faith crisis. Some think walking with God means things will go well in this life, and then the crisis comes. We get cancer at a young age, lose a job, or face some kind of hardship. We have to understand the reality of life in a cursed, fallen world. Walking with God does not mean everything will come up roses. Things do not always work out immediately as they should.

Solomon gives a proverb to explain this situation when he says that what is crooked cannot be made straight and what is lacking cannot be counted (1:15). *Crooked* is a metaphor for sin or moral brokenness in the wisdom literature (Prov 12:8; Job 33:27). Why is the world in this broken state? The world is perverse because of human sin. Ecclesiastes 7:29 makes this clear: "I have discovered that God made people upright, but they pursued many schemes." Humanity has gone its own way against God's design. So because of others' sin and our own sin, we live in a messed-up world, and we can do nothing to fix the situation according to the proverb. It will take a miracle from outside of us to fix what is broken. As Alistair Begg points out, we are trying to line up the squares on the Rubik's Cube with a couple of colors missing ("Word to the Wise")!

When humanity departed from God's design, God imposed a curse on the world (Gen 3; Rom 8). Therefore, everything is broken in our world and in our lives. We try to find ways out of the brokenness but only end up more broken and frustrated. We turn to possessions and pleasurable experiences and status and relationships and even to religion trying to fix what is broken, but it is futile. No amount of pleasurable experiences, job success, or religious ritual can fix what is broken. As we will see, this reality is part of God's goodness in our lives. He imposed the futility in hope that we would long for and hope in Him!

Solomon declares that his wisdom surpassed everyone before him in Jerusalem, but he also says he applied his heart to know madness and folly (1:16-17), which in biblical wisdom literature stands for sin, or the wrong way of life. Solomon was wiser than anyone else, and it did not bring meaning in his life. He also partied harder than anyone else, and that did not work either. That is what he is saying. I tried it all. I lived life the right way (wisdom), and I lived life the wrong way (foolishness), and nothing brought meaning. It was all like trying to grab the wind.

People make sudden shifts in their lives in an attempt to find joy. It reminds me of the Little Caesar's commercial where the guy is having trouble ordering a pizza online, so he screams to his family, "That's it! We're going *off the grid!*" They begin to live an Amish-like existence with no technology, and his wife says, "You should have just gotten a Hot and Ready Pizza from Little Caesar's." To which the husband exclaims, "That's it! We're going back *on the grid!*" People think to themselves that if life were simpler or more elaborate, if I had more stuff or if I had the right relationship, then I would be happy. We keep trying things because we think one change will eventually make all the difference, but it does not. We will see in the following chapters that Solomon denied himself nothing—he indulged every desire and fantasy in an attempt to find satisfaction—and it did not work.

Matt Chandler contrasts the wisdom books of Job and Ecclesiastes. People who are in a Job-like state of suffering think, *If I had more money or better friends, or if I did not have this disease, then life would be better.* But Solomon comes along in Ecclesiastes to destroy that notion ("Sixth Sense"). Here is a guy who had it all, and life was not better. He had all the wisdom in the world, and it only brought him grief (1:18) because he learned through that wisdom that nothing matters. Ignorance had been bliss.

For most of us there was time when we got down on our knees and begged God in prayer for things we now have and take for granted. There was time when we begged God for a spouse, when we begged God for children, when we begged God for a house, and now we have those things and we are still not content. There was a time early in your marriage when you thought to yourself if you could just make $50,000 a year that would be all you would need. You could really be secure. You would not have to fret about finances. Now you make more than that, and you are still not content. The American dream is a lie and a failure. We live in a culture with more money, more entertainment, more pleasurable experiences, more recreation, and more stuff than any previous generation could ever have dreamed, and pain pills and antidepressants fly over the counters of our pharmacies. It's a miserable world where one of the funniest and richest men the world has ever seen—Robin Williams—kills himself in despair.

Ecclesiastes gives a bleak look on life, but the Spirit had a purpose for inspiring this book to be written. He wants to expose the meaninglessness of life in a cursed world in order to create a hunger for something better (Kidner, *Ecclesiastes*, 27). Ecclesiastes wants to push us to faith and contentment in God.

Tim Keller points out that the author drives his readers to see that there are only two possible conclusions in life. Either there is a God above with a standard who will judge us at the end based on that standard, or life is totally meaningless. These are the only two options. Either there is a God and our actions have meaning, or there is no God, and as Hemingway said, "Life is a dirty trick, a short journey from nothingness to nothingness." Keller states, "People think Christians are naive, but if your origin is insignificant, and if your destiny is insignificant, then have the guts to admit that your life is insignificant." Why work for human rights, or for the common good, or for justice for all, if it is all going to be burned up in the end anyway?! If we are just accidents heading for annihilation, then nothing we do matters (Keller, "Problem of Meaning")!

Deep in the human heart we know that is not true—we know what we do matters in some way—but we also know the world is jacked up. Why is it like this? God imposed a curse on the world in response to human rebellion with the purpose that frustration would ultimately drive us to Him. The Holy Spirit inspired Ecclesiastes to convict you of your own meaninglessness in your current existence in order to "make you wise for salvation through Christ Jesus" (2 Tim 3:15 ESV). Romans 8 tells us we are groaning for rescue right along with this frustrated creation! That's exactly what we are directed toward in the conclusion of Ecclesiastes.

Everything Is Meaningless Because Our Frustration Is Meant to Drive Us to Christ
ECCLESIASTES 12:8-14

Ecclesiastes cannot be rightly understood without the conclusion. The bleak outlook of the parts can only be understood in light of the whole that is wrapped up in the conclusion (12:8-14). The conclusion starts with the main point that everything is meaningless by repeating *hevel* as a wrap up (12:8), and then it calls the Teacher a wise man who arranged his writing with great care (12:9). The words of the book are delightful and true (12:10), that is, they give a true portrait of how the world works. His words are like goads (12:11). A goad is a herding tool used to poke and prod livestock in the right direction. The author compares the words of Ecclesiastes with this cattle prod because metaphorically the words of the sage are meant to sting and convict, and thus they move the reader in the right direction of walking in wisdom.

The ultimate Author of Ecclesiastes—the Spirit of God—uses the words of the book to convict the human heart of its need for Jesus. These words are given by "one Shepherd" (12:11). Only three other places in the Bible speak of a single shepherd, and each refers to the Messiah (Ezek 34:23-24; 37:24-25; John 10:11-16) (Perrin, "Messianism," 51–57). Ecclesiastes is therefore a messianic book that points to and longs for the Messiah to come and order His kingdom by wisdom.

Solomon demonstrates this truth even in his closing words to his "son." A sage warning to his son is commonplace in wisdom literature (Prov 1:8; 2:1; 3:1,11). The father—Solomon—wants to train his son—the crown prince—in wisdom. He tells his son that the words of this book are sufficient and should not be transgressed (Eccl 12:12). The son does not need to add to or subtract from them, which is a common statement in the Bible on its sufficiency (see Deut 4:2; Prov 30:6; Rev 22:18-19). Solomon throughout Ecclesiastes has done his own study and experiments to find meaning in this cursed world, and he has come back empty. By telling his son that study is wearisome and there is no end to making books, he is pleading with his son not to go off on his own quest for meaning and satisfaction as if he could try something Solomon did not already try.

Like many parents, Solomon's appeal is, "Do what I say not what I did!" Solomon failed to establish the Davidic kingdom because of his idolatrous lusts, and he pleads with his son for a different outcome. But Solomon's son and all of his descendants would ultimately falter and die. The wisdom literature cries out for a better king who can redeem creation from the curse. Isaiah 11 promises that wise King, and this Greater Solomon is presented to us in Matthew 12. Jesus is the wise King who establishes and orders His kingdom with wisdom—a wisdom that is similar to the wisdom of Proverbs and Ecclesiastes (see the Sermon on the Mount in Matt 5–7).

Solomon's conclusion points forward to Jesus. Solomon says the end of the matter is to fear God and keep His commandments (Eccl 12:13). Indeed, wisdom is tied to keeping the law throughout the Old Testament (Deut 4:6; Ezra 7:14,25). "Trust and obey, for there is no other way to be happy in Jesus, but to trust and obey." Reverent awe and obedience toward God is our obligation because it is the whole duty of mankind. That is God's design for us. Why? The reason to trust and obey is that God will bring every deed into judgment along with every secret thing, whether good or evil (Eccl 12:14). The world is crooked, things are not right, and there needs to be a reckoning to set things right. Ecclesiastes says there will be one. Final judgment is the motivation to trust and obey. Final judgment is what gives every one of our actions meaning in this cursed world. We will be called to account—even for the things we think no one else knows about. Why? God knows, and Jesus says we will answer for every careless word we utter (Matt 12:36-37).

The reality of judgment day is how the Shepherd cares for His flock. In order to convict you, He goads with the truths that you will be judged and then vindicated or punished. The New Testament reveals that the purpose of the law—the purpose of the commandments—is to convict us and bring us to Christ. Solomon and all of his descendants had a problem: they failed and broke the commandments. We have the same problem because we have broken God's commands and sought satisfaction in things and people other than God. You say, "Well, I know I have made mistakes, but I never had a thousand women like Solomon." But you have a harem larger than Solomon on your Internet history (Driscoll, "Setting the Record Crooked"). Ecclesiastes says even the hidden things will be brought to light. We will face judgment, and the bad news is that we have fallen short. This reality is meant to crush us in order to drive us to Christ. That is the good news: Jesus lived the life we could not live, a life without sin in perfect obedience to the commandments, and He died the death we deserved to die. He took the entire curse of sin and futility and death on Himself in order to redeem us from the curse (Gal 3:13). By repenting from our vanity and turning in faith to Him, He redeems us and gives us a new and meaningful life. There is something "new under the sun"—those who are made new creations in Christ (2 Cor 5:17). You will face judgment. You can face it in isolation from Christ and receive God's disapproval, or you can face it in Christ and receive God's approval.

Our lives are broken by sin, but after you receive redemption in Christ, He gives you life everlasting and life to the full now, so that you can recover and pursue God's good design for your life. Now, instead of seeking satisfaction in created things, we are fully satisfied in our Creator, our Redeemer. Satisfied in Him alone you can now rightly enjoy the gifts He gives you as a means to worship Him. You do not need a million dollars. You just need Jesus, and He gives you daily bread (Driscoll, "Setting the Record Crooked"). You do not need to pursue a thousand pleasurable experiences because in Jesus at God's right hand are eternal pleasures (Ps 16:11). Now the seemingly mundane things of life—like scrubbing a dish, working a nine-to-five job, and changing a diaper—are shot through with meaning because Jesus says those who are faithful over the small things are given responsibility over greater things in His kingdom (Matt 25:14-30).

Conclusion

Romans 8:18-21 describes a futile creation that longs for the curse to be overthrown, a creation that longs for resurrection from the dead, and a fallen humanity that screams along with that creation. As Jerome said, what a vanity it is that the earth, which was made for humans, stays while humans dissolve into the dust. The reign of death is strong, and it claimed Adam and Abel and David and Solomon and Rehoboam, and one day it will claim you. But in a world full of grave plots, one grave is empty, and there is one Man whom the dust cannot claim because God would not allow the Holy One to see decay. Jesus is free from the curse, and He graciously offers that freedom to you. Cry out to Him in confession that you have tried to find meaning in something or someone other than Him, and then find your meaning in Him alone (Begg, "Word to the Wise")! As Augustine declared, "Thou hast made us for Thyself, and our hearts are restless until they rest in Thee."

Reflect and Discuss

1. What are some activities you engage in that seem monotonous and unending?
2. What things do you or people you know look to as a means of relieving the redundancy of life?
3. What does *hevel* mean?

4. What New Testament passage seems to be an allusion to *hevel*? What does it refer to there?
5. To what does the phrase "under the sun" refer? How does that limited experience render everything we do meaningless?
6. How does death render everything we do meaningless?
7. Why is the world "crooked"?
8. Why do we always think true happiness will be found in something we lack right now?
9. What is Solomon's purpose in exposing the meaninglessness of life under the sun? Does he achieve his purpose?
10. How does Christ bring significance and meaning to all of our actions, including the ones that seem mundane?

The American Dream Is Meaningless without Jesus

ECCLESIASTES 2:1-26

Main Idea: Pleasure, wisdom, and work are meaningless without Jesus.

I. Pleasure Is Meaningless (2:1-11).
II. Wisdom Is Meaningless (2:12-17).
III. Work Is Meaningless (2:18-23).
IV. Contentment in God and His Gifts Is the Meaningful Life
(2:24-26).

Matt Chandler points out that all of us subscribe to the philosophy that what will ultimately satisfy us is more of what we already have ("Quenched"). For most of us, there was a time when we begged God in prayer for things we now have and take for granted. We prayed for a job, a little better salary, a house, a spouse, and a family; and now that we have those things, we still are not satisfied. You think to yourself, *For me to be happy, I need* _____, and just fill in the blank for your own life: the new iPhone, a new car, a new house, a promotion, a new relationship, and on and on you go. Our entire lives are like this. As a little boy you received a Nintendo one Christmas, and you had the time of your life playing *Mario Brothers, RBI Baseball,* and *Tecmo Bowl,* but then you wore out all those games, had to blow on them ten times to get them to work in the console, and finally got bored with them. Then the Super Nintendo came out, and you got it and loved it for a little while before the Playstation came out. On and on we keep looking to something else to relieve the boredom. As adults the things you want more of change, but the desire for more does not change. Some people sleep on the sidewalk to get their hands on the new iPhone as soon as it comes out. Two years earlier they did the same thing! That phone they could not wait to have has now become a trade-in—if they are lucky enough not to have cracked it.

Nothing ultimately satisfies. We think we "need" more to be happy, but when we accumulate more, we are still not happy. In Ecclesiastes 2, Solomon attempts to expose this philosophy as garbage. He tells us that he had it all and came away empty. Our struggle will be believing Solomon when he says, "I have had it all and done it all, and it was all meaningless." Most of us look at stories of stars who had it all and their life turned out to be a wreck, and we think, *I would trade places with you in a heartbeat. If I had all of that money and fame, I would know how to enjoy it. If I could trade places with the rich and powerful, I would appreciate it more and not make the foolish decisions they made.*

Solomon lovingly attempts to undercut our faulty thinking. In modern vernacular he exposes the emptiness of the American dream. If we would stop for a second, let go of our desire for more and more and more, and look at the many examples around us, we would see that Ecclesiastes 2 is absolutely right. We look at lives like Marilyn Monroe, Kurt Cobain, and Robin Williams, and we see people who had everything this world says you could ever want, and it brought them nothing but pain and emptiness.

That is not just the case for stars on the big scale; it is also true for those around us on the smaller scale. I had a friend in high school who was rich. His dad owned several businesses, and so my friend lived in the nicest house in the nicest subdivision, and he drove the nicest car. We always wanted to stay over at his house on the weekends to swim in his pool and play in his basement. But inevitably, at 2:00 a.m. when we got hungry and crept upstairs to raid the pantry, we would find his mom passed out on the floor next to a wine glass because his dad never came home. His dad never came to his ball games or school plays, and one day his dad said to us, "I know I haven't been around for a whole lot, but that's the decision I made in order to be able to make money and all of this possible." My friend and his family had everything the American dream sells, and they were miserable! Solomon pleads with us not to go that route. He says, "I outdid everyone, and it was all meaningless!"

Pleasure Is Meaningless
ECCLESIASTES 2:1-11

In chapter 1, Solomon concluded that everything is meaningless and fleeting because humanity rebelled against God and now lives in a cursed world where nothing we attempt to build our lives on will ultimately satisfy. If this cursed world is all there is, then there is no profit to all of our activity because nothing changes under the sun. Solomon told us we are trapped in a monotonous prison where nothing changes, and then we die.

That led to Solomon giving his personal testimony about how he tried everything to find some kind of meaning in this life, but he concluded that nothing works. The end of chapter 1 set up Solomon's testimony, and now chapter 2 gives the details to his search for meaning. Like a scientist or a philosopher, he experiments with all kinds of things to see what has lasting value or meaning (Chandler, "Quenched").

First, he turns to pleasure, or what we might call "hedonism." O'Donnell notes, "Within the house of hedonism there are many rooms," and Solomon tries to sleep in them all (*Ecclesiastes*, 43). He adopts the lifestyle of eat, drink, and be merry. Tim Keller points out that it is not until Solomon already concluded that there are no answers in life that he turns to pleasure ("The Search for Pleasure"). If nothing that I do matters and the world is going to burn up in the end, then I need to lighten up. Solomon's attitude is like the guy in the Tim McGraw song who got a bad diagnosis from his doctor and in response did all sorts of crazy things like skydiving, mountain climbing, and riding on a bull. Many people turn to pleasure, if not for ultimate meaning, then for distraction from lack of meaning.

Most of us make our decisions based on what will maximize our pleasure and happiness. We look for what comedian Jerry Seinfeld calls, "little islands of relief in what's often a painful existence" (quoted in Lavery, *Seinfeld*, 158). Solomon's goal is to determine if pleasure provides a solid basis for our lives. Should it be the driving force? Solomon announces his verdict—pleasure is meaningless (2:1)—in advance of the details of his experimentation (Murphy, *Proverbs, Ecclesiastes, Song of Songs*, 184). Pleasure looks like it will make us happy, but it will not. Solomon is in the right position to make this conclusion because he had "epic parties" that fed almost 30,000 people with filet mignon every day.[3] He lived larger than any of us ever could, and he concludes that it was futile.

He turned to laughter and comedy, and he echoes Ecclesiastes 1:3 when he says that laughter and pleasure have no real profit. In fact, laughter is madness. We love comedy movies and passing around funny

---

[3] Mark Driscoll ("Goose Chase") makes this contention based on texts like 1 Kings 4:22-24, but these texts likely refer to the food provisions for his employees, not parties. Either way, much was consumed under Solomon's reign. It was one of opulence and pleasure.

YouTube clips, but laughter cannot provide a basis for life. Quoting comic lines from *Tommy Boy* (1995) and *Dumb and Dumber* (1994) will not build depth into your life or friendships (Eswine, *Recovering Eden*, 67). Alistair Begg points out that comedy is fleeting and does not deal with the weighty matters of life ("Search for Satisfaction"). No one ever walked out of *Billy Madison* (1995) stunned into silence and contemplating life, but they might do that when they walk out of *American Sniper* (2014). Laughter can momentarily distract us from real pain, but it cannot overcome it. So Solomon does not conclude that laughter is evil unless you try to turn it into the solution for life's problems (Garrett, *Proverbs, Ecclesiastes, Song of Songs*, 291).

Begg says that Solomon leaves the comedy club and heads to the bar because he now turns to pleasure in wine (2:3) ("Search for Satisfaction"). Many people turn to substances for pleasure and to cope with life's problems. Proverbs 31 mentions that some use alcohol for this numbing purpose, but Solomon says that way of life is empty.

No doubt beverage alcohol is a controversial topic for many, but let us be honest about what the Bible says. According to the Bible as a whole, and Ecclesiastes in particular, wine can be a joyous thing when used as God intended. Ecclesiastes 9:7 commands, "Drink your wine with a cheerful heart, for God has already accepted your works," and 10:19 states, "A feast is prepared for laughter, and wine makes life happy." On the other hand, the Bible is clear that wine can be bad and evil when used and abused against God's design. The Bible condemns drunkenness as evil, and our experience shows alcohol can be a killer. There is no end to the commercials that show the "joy" alcohol can bring you, but you never see the commercial on Super Bowl Sunday with the party girl hugging the toilet at 3:00 a.m. or the dad pulling off his belt in a drunken rage (Eswine, *Recovering Eden*, 69). The Bible says positive and negative things about alcohol—wine can be used in appropriate or inappropriate ways.

This backdrop sets up Solomon's experimentation here. Scholars disagree about what Solomon's experiment looked like. Some believe the phrase "my mind still guiding me with wisdom" indicates that Solomon did not get drunk (Garrett, *Proverbs, Ecclesiastes, Song of Songs*, 291). Thus, he was a self-controlled connoisseur of fine wine. Others think the phrase "grasp folly" indicates that he did indulge and became sloppy drunk (Enns, *Ecclesiastes*, 43). So the two options are that he was either a wine connoisseur who knew how to pair fine wine with his main course, or he was a frat boy wasting away in Margaritaville. Which is it? In my opinion Solomon did both. I think he says he tried wisdom and folly—he tried every angle—and he came away empty. As Garrett points out, he wanted to find out if drinking and parties were the best solution to the emptiness of life in the face of death, and he concluded that drinking does not take away the pain (*Proverbs, Ecclesiastes, Song of Songs*, 291).

He did this for the purpose of discovering what was good for Adam's sons to do under heaven (2:3). The last phrase of verse 3 is a key phrase. The experiment is intended to find out man's purpose under heaven. Again, Solomon purposefully takes a secular perspective as if this cursed world is all there is. If there is no God and no afterlife, what is best for man to do? Solomon does not take an atheist position; he takes a position of uncertainty. He just cannot know for sure what lies beyond his experience (Keller, "Search for Pleasure"). So what is worthwhile for us in our short years on earth before we die (Longman, *Ecclesiastes*, 89)?

Solomon now lists all the other things he turned to in this search. So many things on this list are the things many of us think would make our lives happy and fulfilling. Look at all his achievements. He built houses (2:4). Solomon built God's house, the temple (1 Kgs 5–6). He built his own palace, which took 13 years and was bigger than the temple (1 Kgs 7:1). He also built houses and shrines for his wives, and he had seven hundred of them (1 Kgs 7:8; 11:3,7). Many people think if they could just have a bigger house in a nicer neighborhood then they will have arrived. Or maybe you want a lake house or a beach house. That is your dream situation. Solomon had all of that and then some! In fact, he built entire cities (2 Chr 8:1-6).

Solomon indulged in the best of architecture, the best of agriculture, and the best of engineering (2:4-6). He planted vineyards, gardens, and parks. Your gardening hobby or the worlds your kids have created in *Minecraft* pale in comparison to Solomon's creations. He constructed an entire irrigation system to water these gardens and parks (2:6). One can still find these pools of Solomon in Israel today. Literally, Solomon tried to create a new garden of Eden (Longman, *Ecclesiastes*, 89). The phrase "every kind of fruit tree in them" (2:5) is used three times in the creation account (Gen 1:11,29; 2:9). He tried to get back to paradise, but one cannot get back there in this fallen world.

Solomon would have been number one on an ancient version of MTV's *Cribs* or *Lifestyles of the Rich and Famous*. He had tons of servants who waited on him hand and foot. Many of you are thinking right now, "Gosh, it would be nice to have a maid to clean the house, a chef to cook my meals, a landscaper to mow my grass, and a stylist to put on my makeup and choose my clothes each day" (Driscoll, "A Goose"). Solomon had all of that.

He had more herds and flocks than any person before him in Jerusalem (2:7). He accumulated an insane amount of silver and gold. The phrase "the treasure of kings and provinces" refers to vassal states that sent Solomon tribute and to the taxation of his own people (Longman, *Ecclesiastes*, 92). Solomon did not just have money; he had military victories and fame because he subdued surrounding nations. He had so much money that silver was as common as stone (2 Chr 9:27). Can you imagine that? In Solomon's day they treated Benjamins the way we treat pennies!

He loved the arts, and he had enough money to buy his own choir (Garrett, *Proverbs, Ecclesiastes, Song of Songs*, 292). He did not have iPods or CD players, but he did not need them because he could buy the band. Some of your daughters would love to buy the band One Direction and have them play whenever it suited them (Driscoll, "A Goose").

Finally, Solomon indulged in sexual pleasure. In addition to 700 wives (1 Kgs 11), he had 300 concubines (cf. Eccl 2:8). A concubine was a woman given to a man simply for the purpose of sexual pleasure. Concubines were objects. Thus, Solomon could out-locker-room-boast basketball all-star Wilt Chamberlain (who once infamously claimed to have been with 20,000 women!) and infamous playboy Hugh Hefner. So many people are on an endless search for sexual pleasure. They may not have a thousand women literally, but they have that many or more in their pornographic Internet history or romance novels. They constantly look for a new illicit experience in order to be satisfied, but like Solomon they come away empty and disappointed—the high only lasts so long.

Solomon concludes his search for pleasure by saying he denied himself nothing (2:10). He had the most success, the best houses, the most possessions, the richest lifestyle, the most sophistication, the finest wines, the most incredible parties and feasts, the greenest lawns, the best servants, more money than we could possibly imagine, military fame, popularity, endless entertainment, and as much sexual pleasure as anyone could ever indulge in, and he says it was all empty (2:11). It led to nothing but brokenness. Incidentally, much of what he detailed is a violation of the kingly laws in Deuteronomy 17 and ultimately cost Solomon's son the kingdom.

Here is the point: He outdid anything we could ever do. Solomon had more and did more than anyone before him (2:9). He indulged in every desire and saw it as the reward for all his efforts (2:10). He concludes that everything was meaningless; he did not gain anything and simply was trying to grab wind (2:11). Even though he played out every one of his fantasies in real life, nothing fulfilled. We think to ourselves that we just need more, and he says, "No! You can accumulate more money, stuff, and partners, but it will not matter!" Nothing brings meaning. If that is true for him, what hope do we have?

When will you be happy? In your mind you say, "I will be happy when _____." What would you put in that blank? Listen to Solomon through the Spirit: it will not work! You think, *If I could just have the American dream, everything would be different and I would be happy*, but when you get it, you are not happy. It is all fleeting and does not satisfy. The state championship, the raise, the new car, and the big house—they all fade!

The cry of this generation is, do not repress your desires because that is dangerous and leads to depression, maybe even suicide. No matter what your desire is, whether it has to do with gender identity, sexual orientation, pleasure, or dreams, do not repress them. Solomon lovingly warns us that indulging in whatever feels good is dangerous. You may get all you ever wanted, but you will not want it when you get it. It will not satisfy. God loves you, and He knows indulging under the sun leads to brokenness. Pleasure is not bad, but because of the fall, it cannot be our final guide. It cannot be ultimate. Pleasure is a *good thing* that if turned into a *god thing* becomes an *enslaving thing*. So, if foolish hedonism does not work, then maybe living the right kind of life will. Right?

Wisdom Is Meaningless
ECCLESIASTES 2:12-17

Solomon now turns to a consideration of wisdom, madness, and folly (recalling 1:17). He starts with a passage that is difficult to translate, but the HCSB says, "For what will the man be like who comes after the king? He will do what has already been done" (2:12). The basic idea is, "Son, don't try to outdo me because you can't." We find the same plea in the conclusion of Ecclesiastes (12:12). Solomon wants his son to learn from his experiments—and his mistakes—so that he does not repeat them. He does not want his son to think, *Oh yeah, well you did not try* _____, *and I will, and I bet I will find meaning in it.* Solomon assures his son that he will end up doing the same things and be in the same place. Solomon tried it all. He lived wisely and foolishly, and none of it worked. We should do what he says, not what he did!

Wisdom has a relatively greater value than foolishness (2:13-14). There is more profit in wisdom than folly just as there is more profit in light than darkness. I usually get up early in the morning while it is still dark outside, and as I get ready. I do not turn any lights on because I do not want to wake anyone else up. One morning as I got out of bed to stumble into the bathroom to get ready, our dog Molly was not in her bed but for some reason was sprawled out on the floor. I did not see her and stepped on her, sending me falling into my dresser and her shooting like a bullet in the other direction. Without light I could not make my way through the house without stumbling. The image here in Ecclesiastes is clear and recalls a similar notion from Proverbs (4:10-19). Wisdom helps you navigate this world without stumbling because it allows you to see clearly the pitfalls, and it allows you to discern the right decision in each situation.

So yes, wisdom is better than foolishness, but the value is only relative, and it does not last. Why? Wisdom's gain over folly is fleeting because both the wise and the fool share the same fate. Death is the great equalizer. That is Solomon's point. What is the use in exerting all of this energy to be wise if this world is all there is and we all end up as worm food in the end? Why deny myself the seeming fun of the foolish life and work hard to be wise when we all end up the same? Death makes meaningless even trying to live the right kind of life in this world.

One might object, "Well, maybe our memory and the good we did in the world can live on." If we live a wise life and leave the world a better place than we found it, then people will at least remember us. Solomon says, "Nope. Even the hope of lasting fame is an illusion" (Garrett, *Proverbs, Ecclesiastes, Song of Songs*, 294). In the ancient story *The Epic of Gilgamesh*, the title character wants to inherit eternal life, but he is told that only Utnapishtim was given that gift. So Gilgamesh heads back home with the intention of building great walls and fortifications to put his name on so he can live on in the monuments he has created (Enns, *Ecclesiastes*, 44). Solomon's point here, which is similar to the

Gilgamesh story, is that there is no way to cheat death, and he should know. He spent years building a beautiful temple, and not one stone of it still stands. Fools and wise alike die, and that renders the effort of wisdom meaningless.

Plus, as an aside—and this is a major issue in Ecclesiastes—wisdom does not always work out immediately. Some say that Ecclesiastes is in tension with the more positive message about wisdom in Proverbs. After all, Proverbs says that a good name will live on (Prov 10:7).[4] However, Proverbs and Ecclesiastes alike are aware that wisdom does not always work out immediately (but it will work out ultimately!). Solomon's struggle of faith in Ecclesiastes is, Why be wise if it does not seem to work in this world? Consider the realm of sports. Every athlete is told the same narrative growing up. Work hard, respect your coach, play by the rules, be a good sport, do not complain about playing time, and show your skills in practice because that is the right way to do things. Yet, in the 2014–2015 NFL season, a guy named LeGarrett Blount smashed that narrative. He was so angry about his lack of playing time with the Steelers that he walked off the field before the game was over. The team cut him the next day, and then the Patriots signed him, and he won a Super Bowl ring. That example is multiplied in our fallen world in every field across the spectrum. Solomon is like a skeptic teetering on the edge of his faith when he sees these kinds of realities. All of us scream for a judgment, a reckoning, beyond the current miserable reality. We want a place where things are set right and folks get what they deserve.

As Solomon looks at how death and the curse render all of our efforts meaningless and empty, he despairs and hates his life (2:17). And yet, there is one more place to look for hope. If we do not live on and our memory does not live on, at least one thing does outlast us. Can we not leave our accumulated wealth as a legacy and an inheritance to our children?

Work Is Meaningless
ECCLESIASTES 2:18-23

Iain Provan calls this section, "The confessions of a workaholic!" (*Ecclesiastes, Song of Songs*, NIVAC, 76). Solomon quickly finds the idea

---

[4] Longman (*Ecclesiastes*, 99) contends that Ecclesiastes cuts against Proverbs.

of work vain. Work is meaningless: we exert all of this effort to amass possessions we never really get to enjoy because we were working all the time, and then we leave them to someone else, and he may be a fool who squanders all we worked to earn! What is the point in working so hard to accumulate so much that we cannot take with us? The cliché is well worn, but you never see a hearse pulling a U-Haul (see 1 Tim 6). We know that, but that truth does not stop us from being workaholics who try to get more, more, more.

In the parable of the rich fool in Luke 12, Jesus warns us about the love of money in light of death taking all we have. A rich man amassed all of these crops and wealth, and he determined to build bigger barns to store them so he could be secure for many years. God says, "You fool! This very night your life is demanded of you. And the things you have prepared—whose will they be?" (Luke 12:20). It is foolish to live your life to accumulate possessions because you do not get to take them with you. No, you have to leave them behind to someone else.

Even the legacy game will not work because eventually your descendants will waste that for which you worked so hard. Statistics say that in 60 percent of cases, inherited wealth is completely gone by the end of the second generation. The fear of billionaires who are "self-made men" is that their spoiled children who never knew hunger will not have the wisdom and resolve to handle so much money. The children of Hall of Fame baseball star Ted Williams tied up so much money fighting over whether to keep him frozen! That is Solomon's point. How long until the family fortune is spent? For Solomon the answer was "quickly"—one generation! First Kings 14:25-26 tells us that a foreign army came into Jerusalem and took Solomon's treasure away from his son Rehoboam. This reality renders work meaningless and only causes despair. Ecclesiastes 2:22 asks the same question as 1:3, and the answer is "nothing" ultimately. There is no net gain from all of our toil.

Solomon will no longer live by the myth that hard work and well-earned wealth validate life (Garrett, *Proverbs, Ecclesiastes, Song of Songs*, 295). Workaholism kills many families in America. Many people are possessed by a restless ambition to achieve, and so they put business before everything else (Greidanus, *Preaching Christ*, 65). They put it before family dinner, before ball games, and before church. Why? Solomon tells us in Ecclesiastes 4:4-6 it is because they want to "keep up with the Joneses." Failure at work or the loss of a job is a hard blow to many, but what is worse than the loss of livelihood is the embarrassment and shame we feel. Envy, the desire to outdo your neighbor, and the longing for recognition are the driving forces for so much restless working. But, as Tim Keller points out, all we really do is plow water. The moment the plow passes, the water fills back in, and there is no evidence we did anything. He points out that the man who created *Strong's Exhaustive Concordance* spent a lifetime cataloging every word in the Bible, and what took him a lifetime to do, we can now do in ten minutes (Keller, "Search for Achievement"). What a waste! Nothing is ultimately gained, and Solomon points out that you even cheat yourself out of rest (2:23). You are never "off" or "home" from work. Your mind is constantly taken up with it. You clock out and come home, and you check your e-mails on your phone all night. You toss and turn while sleep evades you because you stress about the next work project. What futility!

Solomon exposes us to the failure of all his experiments to show us that what he missed in all his efforts was the simple joys God held out to him. All of his experiments failed, so now he finally turns to God. God is gracious to Solomon and us in exposing the failure of everything else to satisfy. God allows us to feel the meaninglessness of our efforts in order to drive us to Him! Ecclesiastes discloses the folly, brokenness, and senselessness of life without God. Like the heart cry of the psalmist in Psalm 73, the pain of death and things not working right in the world drives the true believer to deep satisfaction in God. Our hearts and flesh may fail, but God is the strength of our heart!

Contentment in God and His Gifts Is the Meaningful Life
ECCLESIASTES 2:24-26

Solomon concludes that there is nothing better than to eat, drink, and find enjoyment in toil. These are known as the carpe diem passages, and Solomon says this over and over again: enjoy life, enjoy your wife, eat, drink, work, and be happy (3:12-14; 3:22; 5:18-20; 9:7-10). This is God's gift to man—both the blessings and the ability to enjoy them. Solomon calls the reader to be content and satisfied with God and the gifts from His hand.

In the beginning God designed the world so that we would enjoy the material blessings He gave us as a means to worship Him. As we ate, drank, enjoyed our spouse, and enjoyed our work, it would cause us to thank God for His goodness. But human sin distorted that, so now we look to the created things for the satisfaction only God can give. Not only is this a rebellion against God, but also it renders our true enjoyment of these gifts impossible. We want more, more, more, and we are never happy. We think if we just had a little bit more, then we would be happy, but if we are not happy with what we have right now, then we will not be happy no matter how much we get or experience. More will not satisfy us; only God can.

Again, the problem is not the things in and of themselves but rather the value we place in them. They cannot truly deliver. So be satisfied in the Creator, and then you can rightly enjoy the created things He gives you. As Solomon says, apart from Him there is no enjoyment (2:25). Everything is meaningless without Jesus, but with Jesus we can enjoy everything.

Solomon concludes with the reason for this, and at first blush it might upset some folks.[5] The reason for this reality is that to the one who pleases God, God gives these gifts (wisdom, knowledge, and joy), but sinners—those who go against God's design—are tasked with collecting and collecting in order to give over what they collect to the one who pleases God (2:26). There is no letup or peace for sinners. They are in a meaningless pursuit after the wind. Then, finally, they have to give what is theirs to the one who pleases God. Jesus teaches a similar concept in the parable of the talents in Matthew 25.

Solomon's words raise a question: So you are telling me that God gives good things to good people and takes the things bad people have and gives them to the good people also? Well, sort of! The question, though, that needs to be asked is, Who is the one who pleases God? This verse does not mean God likes good, moral people and gives them nice things. The one who pleases God is not the religious person who tries to do the best he can. Ecclesiastes 12:13-14 tells us it is the one who perfectly obeys God's commandments. The problem for every single one of us is we are sinners, and thus we displease God. Only one person in all of history has perfectly followed God's design and been told of God's pleasure—Jesus. God said of Him, "This is My beloved Son. I take delight in Him!" (Matt 3:17). But by virtue of the gospel, if we will recognize our sin, repent of it, and believe in Jesus, then we are united to Christ by faith so that God no longer sees us in our sin but sees us in union with Christ as His beloved child in whom He is well pleased. In

---

[5] Matt Chandler's sermon "The Gift" was helpful for this section.

Christ God gives you great gifts and now the ability to enjoy them as we are satisfied in Christ!

Despite much of contemporary American Christian thinking, God is not a cosmic killjoy. So many were given the impression growing up that Christianity teaches us to reject the "worldly" view that happiness comes by addition (i.e., adding more money, stuff, and pleasure to your life as Solomon tries in Ecclesiastes 2), and instead the Bible teaches that happiness comes by subtraction (subtract every enjoyable thing from your life because that is what God wants) (Driscoll, "A Goose"). If it feels good, then it is probably a sin, so get rid of it and suppress your desires. Some of you may even be thinking that this sermon is another example. *Oh great! Another sermon where I'm told to be miserable. You're telling me that all of those pleasures Solomon mentioned and all of that education and all of that work—those are all bad things. I should not want a house or a car or money or sex or any of those things. I just get to be miserable?* No! That is not Christianity. Not one of those things Solomon mentioned is necessarily evil. Music, laughter, gardening, sex with your spouse, and all of those other things can be good and holy if used as God intended. The problem is we revolted against God, so now we are broken. But in Christ we are redeemed to recover and pursue God's design for our lives, which includes enjoying the material gifts He has given to us.

Conclusion

Solomon's life in so many ways reminds us of the prodigal son (Luke 15). So many think the prodigal son's sin was partying too much, and then he came to his senses and wanted to leave his party days behind. We so often forget the story does not just begin with partying; it ends with partying. Yes, there's a party in the far country that leaves the son broken, but there is also an epic party when he gets back home. Dancing and singing can be heard outside. The difference is the son cannot enjoy the party rightly until he is satisfied in the father's love.

That is the gospel of Jesus Christ. Satisfied in Christ and His love, we now can enjoy life, marriage, children, work, laughter, gardening, building, and so many other pursuits as God intended! As C. S. Lewis reminds us, our problem is not that we desire too much; it is that we desire too little. When we pursue created things at all cost, we settle for cardboard pizza at Chuck E. Cheese's instead of enjoying a night at Ruth's Chris when we are satisfied in Jesus! We live in a Genesis 3:19 world where dust returns to dust, and we long for Genesis 3:15 to come true. David died, and he decayed. Solomon was a backslidden king who decayed into the dust. But one Son of David did not dissolve into the dust. He walked away from the tomb, ascended into heaven, and boldly took his seat at God's right hand where Psalm 16 says there are pleasures that last forever. Do you want pleasures that last forever and are not fleeting? In Christ we are already raised from the dead and seated in the heavenly places (Eph 2:4-6). So enjoy life now and forever.

Reflect and Discuss

1. What do you and the people around you think is necessary to be truly happy?
2. Why do we continue to think possessing more than we have right now will make us happy when we are not happy with what we have?
3. Why do pleasurable experience and the accumulation of money and things not ultimately satisfy?
4. In what practical ways does a life of wisdom make more sense than a life of foolishness? If this life is all there is, think through how those advantages are canceled.
5. Why do most of us kill ourselves to succeed in work despite the Bible's repeated warnings that we do not get to take our stuff with us when we die?
6. Were you given the impression growing up in church that pleasure was to be avoided? Why do you think that was what you were taught?
7. What do we often think we need to do for God to be pleased with us? What does the Bible say is the path to God's pleasure?
8. What are some ways we use pleasure, possessions, relationships, and work in ways God did not design?
9. What are some ways we can enjoy pleasure, possessions, relationships, and work in ways God did design?
10. How can we fight against finding satisfaction in created things and instead find it in God alone?

Time Is Meaningless without Jesus

ECCLESIASTES 3:1-15

Main Idea: Because we are trapped in time, we should trust the eternal God's plan and enjoy His gifts.

I. **If This Cursed World Is All There Is, Then Time Is Meaningless (3:1-9).**

II. **Your Frustration Should Drive You to Trust Christ (3:10-15).**

"God wrote a pop song" (Begg, "Eternity on My Mind"). Pete Seeger and the Byrds made Ecclesiastes 3 famous in pop culture with the hit, "Turn! Turn! Turn!" All but six words of the song come straight from the biblical text, which is why Pete Seeger sends a portion of his royalties to Israel (*Wikipedia*, "Turn! Turn! Turn!"). The catchy tune comforts many people who think to themselves, *It doesn't matter how bad things get; good times are coming!* Life ebbs and flows, and if I am in a bad season now, then good times are just around the corner.

But the comfort of "Turn! Turn! Turn!" does not accurately communicate Solomon's mood or intention in Ecclesiastes 3. "Time" by Hootie and the Blowfish better communicates Solomon's message because in that song time haunts rather than comforts. After all, the song talks about time as a punishment. The song says terrorizing things about time, like the fact that it crushes dreams, causes tears to fall, brings all kinds of pain and sadness into your life, and is an enemy rather than a friend. Time does not comfort; time haunts because it is fleeting and filled with sorrow that cancels out joy. Like watching sand run through the hourglass, you watch your life run out. As Isaac Watts reminds us, "Time, like an ever rolling stream, bears all its sons away" ("Our God, Our Help in Ages Past").

We feel this tension and foreboding in our own lives. It is revealed to us in phrases like, "Where did the time go?" "There aren't enough hours in the day." "I've got to make the most of my time." "When will my time come?" (Eswine, *Recovering Eden*, 126). For some, most likely those in adulthood, time moves way too fast. The moment you begin to figure out and enjoy one season, you are on to the next one. Time will not slow down for you to enjoy anything. Each year passes more quickly than the last. For others, most likely the young, you are frustrated by the slowness of time. You cannot wait for more freedom, for your driver's license, to be done with school, or to be out on your own. Time frustrates all of us. Why is that? What should we do about it? Let us look to God's Word in Ecclesiastes 3:1-15 for the answer.

If This Cursed World Is All There Is, Then Time Is Meaningless
ECCLESIASTES 3:1-9

So far in Ecclesiastes, Solomon has taught that if this cursed world is all there is, then all of our actions in this life are futile. We do things that don't matter, and then we die. In that reality nothing in which you look for meaning, and nothing you turn to in to distract yourself from the harsh realities of life, really works. Pleasure will not satisfy human longings; neither will wisdom or work or a lot of money or any of the things we expend so much energy chasing. Solomon's purpose is to expose the foolishness of a life lived without God in order to push us to enjoy God and His gifts. Satisfaction in God and His gifts is the meaningful life. The Spirit's ultimate point in inspiring Ecclesiastes is to teach us that everything is meaningless unless you have Jesus. The time poem in Ecclesiastes 3 is another example to prove Solomon's thesis that life "under heaven" is futile and fleeting.

Again, Solomon limits his observations to this present world when in Ecclesiastes 3:1 he states that for everything there is an occasion and a time for every activity under heaven. An occasion is a period of time in which certain activities take place. For example, winter is the period for snow, ice, and below-zero wind chills. Thus, the text states that there is an appointed time or season for every activity, and life moves from one season to the next. My son, Judson, is 17 months old, and it is perfectly appropriate for him to be pushed around the supermarket in a shopping cart, but if he is 17 years old and doing the same thing, then there is a major problem. We move from one season to the next as we grow up. Begg points out that a cycle to life is inevitable. When you were in high school and saw what the "rat race" did to your dad, you said to your buddy that you would never grow up and get a nine-to-five job, you would never wear a suit, and you would never settle down. But 20 years later you sit at lunch break from your nine-to-five job with your friend, both wearing suits and saying to each other, "How did we ever end up here?" (Begg, "Eternity on My Mind"). Life moves from one season to the next and one activity to the next.

The poem describes these activities, but it does not remark on them. It does not evaluate them as good or bad, wise or foolish, righteous or sinful. Each could be appropriate, but that is not his concern. Solomon merely describes the seasons of life; he does not prescribe what we should do. He does not tell you how to capture the positive things on the list and avoid the negatives (Garrett, *Proverbs, Ecclesiastes, Song of Songs*, 297). The poem does not teach Proverbs-like wisdom to discern which is the right season for which activity. That is not Solomon's intention. He merely describes the full scale of life's activities on earth. He moves through 14 pairs of opposites. Matching opposites is a poetical device known as "merism," which not only makes statements about the two extremes but also everything in between them. For example, one common biblical merism is "heaven and earth" which does not mean simply the ground and the sky but everything in creation. Thus, these 14 opposite pairings are meant to paint a complete picture of reality and life on earth (Enns, *Ecclesiastes*, 52). The picture is of the impermanent and mortal nature of life (Kidner, *Ecclesiastes*, 38). The poem gives the full range of human and natural experiences: birth, work, love, war, peace, and death.

There is a time to give birth and a time to die (3:2). These are the bookends of life under the sun, and everything else mentioned in the poem falls between them. This statement is another reminder of the frailty of life, and it recalls the endless cycle of the generations in 1:14. One generation dies, then another comes on the scene. That generation dies, and then another comes, and on and on it goes. Death is pervasive in a post-Genesis 3 world. And as Genesis 5 points out, there are always new generations, and they ultimately die as well. People sometimes look to Ecclesiastes 3 for comfort at funerals, and people will even sometimes say, "Death is just part of the cycle of life." That may be true since the fall, but that is not how it was originally supposed to. God created life, and death is an enemy that reminds us we live in a cursed world. Not only does human life end, but so does plant life. There is a time to plant and to pluck up (3:2). You poured sweat and got your hands dirty planting that tomato garden. But eventually a season comes with an untimely frost or a lack of rain, your plants die, and you have to root them out.

There is a time to kill and heal (3:3). Kill can refer to appropriate forms like self-defense, just war, or capital punishment. In the context it might naturally refer to an agricultural setting. The farmer nurses an injured animal back to health, only to have to put the same animal down later. We have a pastor friend named Clint who told us about an unusual experience in the first church he pastored. It was in a small town in Mississippi, and he had one deacon, who was a farmer. He called Clint one day and said, "Pastor, I need your help. My favorite cow is sick and needs to be put down, but I don't have the heart to do it. Can you come do it?" Even though that was not something Clint learned to do in seminary, he agreed and went to the farm. The deacon sat on the porch holding a shotgun, which he handed to Clint. He said, "The cow is up over that hill. Just walk on down there, put the shotgun right behind her ear, pull the trigger, and that will be it." So Clint said, "You just stay right here, and I will go take care of it." Clint walked over the hill and down to where the cow was lying on the ground. He put the shotgun behind the cow's ear, pulled the trigger, and the cow jumped up and started bucking. So, "Boom! Boom! Boom! Boom!" several more shots rang out. Clint walked back up to the house, and the deacon said, "What was all that commotion?" Clint said, "That cow was not as sick as you led me to believe!" That is part of the cycle of life. The animal you heal one day needs to be put down.

Now, remember that these are descriptions of reality not prescriptions for what to do. Your takeaway from this message is not "I need to go kill someone, and I have a working list ready." People hear all kinds of things that preachers do not say, so let's be clear. Ecclesiastes 3 is not a license to kill.

Not only is there a time to kill and heal; there is also a time to break down and build up (3:3). The houses previous generations poured their hearts and all their money into building are eventually condemned, torn down, and cleared for something else to be there.

There is a time to weep and laugh, and there is a time to mourn and dance (3:4). We live in a cursed world full of marriages and funerals. You get married, dance at the reception, rejoice when someone gets pregnant to start a family, and then find out they miscarried. That is life under the sun. David danced before the Lord in great joy when the ark came to Jerusalem (1 Chr 15:29), and he cried deeply at his son's sickness (2 Sam 12:15-23) (Eswine, *Recovering Eden*, 135). There are moments of joy and levity, and there are moments of deep pain.

There is a time to cast away and gather stones (Eccl 3:5). The phrase is difficult to understand for modern ears, but most likely stone casting refers to an ancient war practice. For example, 2 Kings 3:19,25 lays out a war strategy for Israel in which they are to cast stones on their enemies' fields in order to make them unworkable. It disrupts agriculture. Isaiah 5:2 describes the process of clearing stones from a field before you plant a vineyard.

There is also a time to embrace and refrain from embracing (Eccl 3:5). There are times when you greet friends with a hug, and there is a time to sever friendships. When I (Jon) was in high school, I had great friends, and I thought we would be close forever, but my dad (Danny) cautioned me by saying, "Most people do not remain close with their high school friends." He was right. Life moves on, you move to different places, and other relationships come. These are the facts of life.

There is a time to seek and lose (3:6). When you lose something, you look hard to find it, but a time comes when you have to give up the search. I am convinced the Bermuda Triangle is located somewhere inside our house because we lost two remote controls years ago, and despite our best search efforts, we have never found them. When our girls lose a toy and get real upset, we say, "Don't worry. It's in the house somewhere. We will find it." But then we look at one another and quietly say, "Unless it's in the same place as the remotes." There is a time to continue looking and a time to stop. There is a time to keep and a time to cast away (3:6). You have a picture your daughter made in kindergarten. It might look like junk to everyone else, but it is a treasure to you, so you hold on to it. But it might be time to consign those clothes you keep thinking you will eventually fit back into or at least take them to Goodwill (Driscoll, "Peering over the Loom"). There is a time to store and a time for garage sales.

There is a time to tear and sew (3:7). Most likely this statement refers to the Jewish practice of tearing your garment in times of grief, mourning, or repentance (Hunt, *Ecclesiastes*, 12). For example, when Jacob thought a predatory beast had killed Joseph, he tore his clothes (Gen 37:29). But when the time of mourning ended, then it was time to sew up the garment. There is also a time to keep silence and a time to speak (Eccl 3:7). The phrase might refer to the wisdom practice of discerning the right time to confront or refrain as outlined in places like Proverbs 26:4-5 (Longman, *Ecclesiastes*, 117). Sometimes you confront the fool; other times you refrain. There is a time to confront people, and there is a time to be silent, praying and hoping they will repent (Driscoll, "Peering over the Loom").

There is a time to love and hate, and there is a time for war and peace (3:8). The author moves from personal experience to national experience (Longman, *Ecclesiastes*, 117). Again the poem does not advocate war or pacifism. It simply describes part of the human experience. For example, a country like Japan that has a foreign policy of pacifism begins to rethink its policy when ISIS beheads a Japanese journalist in 2015. It is inevitable that peaceful nations will eventually be pulled into conflict.

The point of the poem is the inevitable sameness and monotony of life under the sun. We all go through these actions of birth, life, work, love, and then death. Nothing really changes for humanity. Meaninglessness in life and death in the end pervade our experience in this cursed world. Here today and gone tomorrow. This is just the way it is.

We see this truth reinforced as Ecclesiastes 3:9-15 comments and reflects on the poem. Ecclesiastes 3:9 restates the question of Ecclesiastes 1:3—What gain is there in this reality? What profit or advantage is there in this world where God has imposed a curse on our toil and activities (see Gen 3:17-19)? The answer is nothing. There is no purpose to life because everything we do is nullified by the curse. There is no net gain or change from all the planting, building, and warring. There is just more work to do, more dishes to clean, more wars to fight with no lasting peace, and all of it ends in death. The poem in Ecclesiastes 1:3-11 makes this case in nature with its endless but profitless cycles, and now Solomon makes the same point about human activity, both realities being set by God (Enns, *Ecclesiastes*, 52).

The poem reveals the great absurdity of life because each activity cancels the other out. There are 14 pluses and 14 minuses, and that adds up to zero (Begg, "Eternity on My Mind")! Every birth ends in death, every planted crop is pulled up, every building is eventually condemned, every celebration gives way to a funeral, and every peace gives way to another war. Nothing is gained.

I saw this reality clearly in my family life. Our family had a humongous Great Dane named Samantha. She was a wonderful dog, but she came near death several times in her life. She ate gauze, and it wrapped around her intestines. Surgery saved her life. Then she ate my mom's panty hose, it wrapped around her intestines, and surgery saved her life. Finally we left her in a kennel when we went on Christmas vacation to Georgia, and she got pneumonia. The vet had to put her in a doggy oxygen tent to save her life. My dad did with Samantha something he would have sworn earlier in life that he would never do. He spent thousands of dollars saving that dog's life! But do you know what happened? Samantha eventually had serious injuries to her back knees so she could not walk. My parents would have to carry her outside to go to the bathroom, and eventually she would just mess herself. So they had to call the vet to come put her down. Through tears they spent their last moments with her giving her things to eat that she liked but was not supposed to have, like chocolate (and tissues—for some reason!). They spent thousands saving her life, but eventually she had to be put to sleep.

Life is a big nonplus. We seek meaning in all of our activities and come away frustrated. What do we do? Where do we turn in this frustration? The frustration of our current existence should drive us to fear God.

Your Frustration Should Drive You to Trust Christ
ECCLESIASTES 3:10-15

Ecclesiastes 3:10 restates 1:13, and thus it gives a negative evaluation to the poem of 3:1-9. God imposed a curse on creation because of Adam's rebellion, so now we experience burdened toil. Activity and work were not designed to be frustrating, but they are now in a cursed world. Our frustration is therefore a God-enforced burden. But why? What is the purpose? We see God's intent in the following verses.

Ecclesiastes 3:11 is an extremely difficult verse to understand. People love the verse and quote it, but they only quote part of it. I am not sure they understand what it means. We will walk through each of the three clauses separately to see what they say, and then we will attempt to put them together to see the whole and how it connects with the negative tone that led to this point.

God made everything beautiful—or perhaps it is better to say "appropriate"—in its time. "Time" calls us back to the poem to show that the author is now commenting on these times. The phrase "He has made" refers to God's initial act of creation, but it can also refer to everything He has done since the creation (Longman, *Ecclesiastes*, 119). The word translated "beautiful" or "appropriate" means God made everything good and right, so that everything perfectly fits its own place and time.

Bottom line, the phrase sums up the poem to show that God is the One in charge of these times and appointed activities. And it sets up what follows. The overarching point seems to be that God has appointed or ordained all of these things as part of His bigger, hidden plan.

The next phrase famously says that God has put eternity into people's hearts. Eternity here contrasts with "time," which was used 29 times in the poem (Greidanus, *Preaching Christ*, 72). We know that life under the sun is not all there is, thus it is absurd to live as if this life is all there is. There is a desire to live forever; there is a desire for more than life under the sun, and there is knowledge of an eternity out there beyond this life.

The final—often-ignored—phrase of Ecclesiastes 3:11 gives the problem: "But man cannot discover the work God has done from beginning to end." We cannot know or see God's entire plan or fully grasp it, no matter how much we want to. The limit of man's knowledge is a major theme in Ecclesiastes, and the purpose of exposing that reality is to drive us to faith in God. We know there is more out there, and we want to know our purpose and our destiny. However, we are still dependent creatures who can only know and handle a sliver of what the Creator is really doing. And if we doubt in any way the truth of that statement, we need to be reminded that, mysterious as it may be, when the Son of God set aside His glory and took on human flesh, even He did not know all the times set by God (Matt 24:36). As Matt Chandler points out, we are like a child in the "why stage" ("Ingredients"). When you tell a child in the why stage to do something, he or she can ask "Why?" into infinity, and eventually you have to say in exasperation, "Because I told you so." In a sense we cannot handle all of the whys of God's plan, so He tells us, "Even though you cannot know it all, you can trust Me!"

Here, then, is the main idea of 3:11 and how it fits with the absurdity of life described earlier. We perceive and long for better things than this cursed misery, but we cannot see the full picture, and we must lean on God. We are trapped between time and eternity, and we must trust that God uses the details to work out a grander plan.

Perhaps my favorite movie series is the Star Wars franchise, especially the original trilogy. Imagine if you had no prior knowledge of that series, and I took you into a movie theater and showed you the final scene from *The Empire Strikes Back* (1980). I showed you the fight between Darth Vader and Luke Skywalker. I showed you the revelation that Darth Vader is Luke's father, to which Luke screams like a baby,

"Nooooo!" I showed you Darth Vader cutting off Luke's hand with a lightsaber and then Luke falling down the tunnel and the rebellion retreating. Then I shut the movie off. You would be perplexed and confused, but you would also inherently know there was a bigger plot and story line at play. You would know that there is a backstory you are missing, and you would want to see what happens next because you would inherently know that could not be the end of the story. You had only been shown a sliver of what the director/storyteller was doing in his grand masterpiece. The pain of the few moments I showed you would not make much sense. If later on you got to see the end, and you got to see how in *Return of the Jedi* (1983) Darth Vader turns away from the dark side of the force and rescues his son from the murderous emperor, then all of the painful details would fall into place. You would see how they were part of a masterpiece that worked out well in the end. There is a resolution that your heart yearned for.

That is the frustration Solomon feels but also the confidence that something more is going on. We have a small vantage point. We are frustrated because we cannot get past the fragmentary image to see the whole picture. We want our lives to matter, and we try to find ways to make that happen. We look to all kinds of pleasures, experiences, relationships, and possessions in vain hopes of making sense of things. But we need to understand a divine purpose and plan were set in motion at the beginning and will work out in the end. There is a sovereign God reigning over all things who not only sees all that will happen but declares all that will happen.

You were made for the Divine and for His purpose, so there should be no surprise that you get frustrated when you turn away from Him. That is the frustration Solomon has been exposing throughout the book. God wants you to be dissatisfied until you come to fellowship with Him. And you will never be satisfied without Him (Begg, "Eternity on My Mind"). Augustine famously put it this way: "You made us for Yourself, and our hearts are restless until they can find their rest in You."

This tension leads to another carpe diem passage in which Solomon encourages us to enjoy the details of our lives because they are part of this beautiful picture. He says there is nothing better for Adam's sons than to enjoy good things as long as they live (3:12). Your life is a fleeting mist, so enjoy it while you can. Eat, drink, and enjoy your work because this is God's gift to man (3:13). As Solomon said in chapter 2, enjoyment of life is a gift that God gives to the one "who is pleasing in His sight" (2:24-26). Again the question must be asked, Who pleases God? The answer is that none of us do because we have all sinned, but Jesus Christ is the well-pleasing Son who never sinned but took God's wrath against our sins on the cross, so that by means of faith we might become pleasing and acceptable to God through Jesus Christ. Therefore, only those who believe the gospel can rightly enjoy God's blessings as God intended instead of turning the blessings into idols.

Resting in Christ and being reconciled to God through Him, we are satisfied in the Creator and enjoy, rather than worship, created things. So drink deeply of life as a gift from God. Cuddle your children, learn to fish, hit a golf ball, teach a class, eat a fattening dessert, work out, spend time with your family, and so much more as a means of worshiping your Creator (Driscoll, "Peering Over the Loom" and Chandler, "Ingredients"). Our middle daughter Emma will say to us from time to time, "I'm so thankful to be part of this family." Solomon says to drink deeply of those moments because they do not last forever. Enjoy everything that is happening around you as part of the loving plan of your heavenly Father.

Solomon concludes by saying that whatever God does endures forever (3:14). Nothing can be added to or subtracted from God's work in the world. God's plan cannot be changed, and He has a specific purpose for His plan and even the frustration we feel. It is to cause people to revere Him. This is key in Ecclesiastes. The fear of God is the beginning of wisdom, and it is the key to alleviating the frustrations of life trapped between time in this cursed existence and eternity. There is no use trying to change the past, the present, or the future. God uses all of this tension, frustration, and burden to drive us to Him. It is a sign of God's goodness. He knows there is no such thing as happiness apart from Him, and He wants us to learn that.

Some might object, "I don't like that." We do not like the limit of human knowledge or the mystery around what God is doing. Some may even say, "Why will God not make Himself more clearly known?" Begg replies, "God is under no obligation to cater to your intellectual curiosity. You cannot pull a string and make God dance for you. He only caters to the contrite of heart" ("Eternity on My Mind"). We must revere Him!

Christians love Romans 8:28 and the promise that God works all things together for the good of those who love Him and are called according to His purpose. But Paul assures us that means we will experience famine, peril, nakedness, and other pains. God uses all of these to conform us into the image of Christ (Rom 8:29). So Solomon and Paul call us to trust God and be confident that His plan is good. He knows all of your days, and He is sovereign over the details and seasons of your life. He mixes the good and the bad—the joys and the pains—together to make something beautiful. We often do not like that. We would rather pick and choose. Let me have the good only, Lord, and none of the bad! He does not allow us to pick and choose because He loves us too much to allow us to turn into Veruca Salt (Chandler, "Ingredients"). She is the girl from *Willie Wonka and the Chocolate Factory* (1971) whose daddy caters to her every desire. She wants the golden goose, and if she does not get what she wants, then she will scream and pitch a fit. God loves us too much to allow us to become spoiled brats. He uses both pleasure and pain as part of His plan to conform us into the image of Christ.

Now some of you may be thinking, as you look from your earthly vantage point, *How could what happened to me ever be beautiful? Not that! Not what happened to me.* God lovingly tells us we are too close to see the big plan, but we can trust Him. He has us, and He has your pain that seems like a jagged piece of glass, and He says that once you can step back and see the stained-glass window, you will see that it is gorgeous (Chandler, "Ingredients"). Yes, it hurts, but yes, God has you, and you can trust Him.

This reality shoots our life through with meaning. God does not abandon one second of our life under the sun (Eswine, *Recovering Eden*, 134). He fits each part—even the smallest of parts—into the whole. This is the God who turns evil into good. This is the God of Joseph, a man who was betrayed by his brothers, sold into slavery, and wrongfully imprisoned, but who then became a ruler in Egypt. God used all of the mess that happened to Joseph to put him in a position to save the world from famine. When his brothers were afraid he would exact his revenge now that he had a position of power and their father Jacob was dead, he said to them, "You planned evil against me; God planned it for good to bring about the present result—the survival of many people" (Gen 50:20).

While we live in this cursed existence east of Eden and long for the Redeemer promised in Genesis 3:15 and hope to once again have access to the tree of life, we know something better is out there. And in this context the Bible tells us about our God, that "when the time came to completion" (Gal 4:4), God sent His Son Jesus into this cursed world to experience all of the times and seasons that we do. There was a time for Jesus to be born, a time for Him to heal the sick, a time for Him to build up, a time for Him to tear down long-held structures, a time for Him to party with sinners, a time for Him to weep at his friend's grave, and a time for Him to die. He entered into this miserable world to take on all of its pain and suffering. He took the curse on Himself so that God could turn the evil of the cross—wicked men murdering the Son of God—into the salvation of the world. Romans 8 tells us our lives fit into this same plan, where joy and pain ultimately bring us into conformity with Christ.

Conclusion

Ecclesiastes 3 says that God appointed the seasons, and Ephesians 1:10 tells us that all things will be summed up in Christ. There is a reason God wove the seasons into the fabric of creation. There is a reason why there are seedtime and harvest. There is a reason there are winter and spring, and it is not so that we do not get bored. God created the seasons to point us to Christ. So when we look outside in the literal dead of winter at trees with no leaves and barrenness all around, we know that in a few months or even weeks everything will spring to life again. God wove winter and harvest into the fabric of creation to show humanity that Jesus would be raised from the dead and make all things new. All of the times of our lives and the seasons point us to find our rest in Him because He is the One working out the ultimate plan to make all things new!

Perhaps "Turn! Turn! Turn!" did not get the feel of Solomon's words just right, but they did get the final note right. They end where Solomon's poem ends, with "Shalom," and they say it is not too late. Indeed! May the Prince of Peace come and set all things right.

Reflect and Discuss

1. In what ways do you find the seasons of your life comforting? In what ways are they concerning?
2. Do you feel that time is moving too fast or too slow? Why?
3. Is there something you do or experience in life right now that earlier in your life you promised you would never do? What might that be?
4. Even though we do not typically live in an agricultural setting today, what are some ways our lives mirror the times in verses 2-8?
5. In what ways do you feel you are spinning your wheels?

6. What are some indicators in our life that we were made for more than time and were meant for eternity?

7. Were there trying times in your life that you did not understand at the time, but as you look back, you can see God's good purpose in all of it? What were they, and how did God use them?

8. How can you trust God during painful times that you do not understand and cannot possibly see how they might be used as part of His plan?

9. How does knowing that God has a grand plan help you enjoy life now? What are some things you need to enjoy more deeply in light of that reality?

10. How can the fact that Christ experienced the same frustrations we feel help us deal with difficulties in our lives?

Politics and Justice Are Meaningless without Jesus

ECCLESIASTES 3:16–4:3 AND 5:8-9

Main Idea: The meaninglessness of justice and politics in this cursed world cries out for a Savior.

I. Justice Is Meaningless (3:16-17).
II. We Receive Death for Our Part in the Sin and Injustice of the World (3:18-22).
III. Politics Is Meaningless (4:1-3,13-16; 5:8-9).
IV. Ecclesiastes Cries Out for a Better King, a Resurrection, and a Final Judgment (12:12-14).

Why am I here? What's the reason for my existence? Those are gigantic questions. Most people know things like pleasure or possessions or the pursuit of money are not high enough values. Most of us recognize that those aims are too low and inadequate for life. There has to be more to life—something more meaningful—than money and pleasurable experiences. As people ask the question about the meaning of life and come to believe that they are here for a "higher purpose," many conclude, "I am here to make the world a better place."

People try different routes to accomplish that purpose. Some people go the route of politics. That is the path "cultural Christianity" has chosen. They put their hope in politics. That was the narrative I was raised on as the Moral Majority wedded evangelical Christianity to hope in the government. There was a lot of preaching on politics and even the end times, and the message was that America was going to receive God's judgment if we did not return to the faith of our founding fathers. It was determined that the path to reaching that return was electing the right people who would pass the right laws. We were told that if we could elect the right people who would pass the right laws, then America would be blessed again.

That was the path I gravitated to both personally and professionally. The first time I was ever published was in a book of poetry in the sixth grade in which I wrote a poem about abortion and called pro-choicers

48

"liberal rats." I was passionate about politics, so passionate that I initially chose that career path. I entered the University of Kentucky as a political science major hoping to change the world through politics. But God ultimately had a different path for me, and one of the ways He accomplished that was causing me to become jaded with the political process. I looked over the course of my life and saw that there were times we had a conservative president, a conservative Congress, and a mostly conservative Supreme Court, and yet nothing really changed. Even recently, in 2015, once the conservatives won back the congress, the pro-life congressmen and women tabled a bill on late-term abortions for the sole purpose of currying favor with female voters. There was an opportunity to push for real change, but being electable won out over defending the defenseless unborn. These realities jaded me, and they revealed to me that politics ultimately does not change the world.

Many people are jaded with politics and think that nothing really changes, so they choose a different route to find meaning in life by changing the world. The second option is grassroots work for social justice. People fight against the system in order to see real change. They work to help the poor, defenseless, and disenfranchised. Many young people—who cannot seem to clean their rooms—desire to clean up the world, and so they gravitate to this path. They get excited, and rightly so, about causes like orphan care, sex trafficking, endangered animals, and the environment. Some work hard to make a difference, but let's be honest, in most cases there is little actual change. Just look at recent news reports that claim the Red Cross overpromised and way underdelivered on compassion efforts in Haiti, where some allege the charity raised half a billion dollars and yet only built six homes despite pledges to rebuild entire communities (Sullivan, "In Search").

That is Solomon's point in Ecclesiastes. If this cursed world is all there is, then all of our actions, even actions to promote the common good, are futile. In Ecclesiastes 3:16–4:3 and also 5:8-9, Solomon indicts both politics and justice as ultimately fleeting and meaningless.

Justice Is Meaningless
ECCLESIASTES 3:16-17

Solomon has made the point throughout Ecclesiastes that if this cursed world is all there is, then nothing you attempt to find meaning in will satisfy and work. His purpose in pointing this reality out is to expose the foolishness of trying to live life without God in order to drive us to enjoy God and His gifts. Now Solomon's discussion of time in Ecclesiastes 3:1-15 leads into a discussion of politics and justice.

This passage actually starts with a heading in Ecclesiastes 3:15c, whose translation is much debated. Literally the text should read, "God seeks the persecuted" (Garrett, *Proverbs, Ecclesiastes, Song of Songs*, 300–301). What does God seek? He seeks justice for the persecuted, which means He will hold the persecutors accountable. Since, as Solomon has stated, there is a time for everything in God's plan, Solomon acknowledges that there is a time to judge the wicked for their role in injustice in the world. The problem with history is that there is not only little or no progress (3:1-15), there is also little or no justice (3:16–4:3) (Keller, "Problem of History"). This is the background to the current passage.

Solomon looks to the place where justice and righteousness should be—the courts—and instead sees wickedness. In this cursed existence, even where you should find things made right, there is injustice. What does this mean? It means the innocent are found guilty and the guilty are acquitted. The rights of the poor and defenseless are not protected (which was a key function of the authorities in the Old Testament). Isaiah 5:23 acknowledges that this was a problem in Israel—the guilty were acquitted for a bribe. Whether one was guilty or innocent was not the deciding factor but rather how much money a person had.

While we would like to think things are different in modern America, they really are not. The rich can get away with murder if they can afford the right defense team. There is a person who works at LifeWay right now who spent decades in jail for a crime he did not commit. He was exonerated by DNA evidence that showed he was never at the crime scene. But his life was torn apart. We live in a world where a thief can fall through the roof of a house he is attempting to rob, sue the homeowner, and win a settlement. Our system often is less about justice and more about having the right lawyer and having the right money (Driscoll, "Gift of Death"). We view this reality and are outraged, and rightly so. There needs to be accountability. Things need to be set right, but that does not happen!

People are pained over this reality. Children do not get far into life without uttering the phrase, "That's not fair," to which we parents respond, "Life's not fair." And that is true. Life is not fair. But something deep inside of us says that it should be. That is why songs like John Lennon's "Imagine" and John Mayer's "Waiting for the World to Change" endure. We long for justice because we were made in the image of a God who is just. We wonder, When will God do something about this? When will things be made right? When will ISIS pay for crucifying children? Beheading innocents? When will the sex traffickers get what's coming to them? We recognize that there needs to be a final and ultimate accountability. After all, if there is not a final reckoning, then the 9/11 hijackers never got what they rightfully deserve. They received the same fate as the people they killed. We cannot accept that as reality, and for good reason: it is not. The Bible cries out for this as well. We watch in the news that ISIS beheaded 21 of our Egyptian brothers, and we cry out with the martyrs in Revelation 6, "How long until You judge and avenge our blood from those who live on the earth?"

Solomon answers this cry. He says that there is a set time for God to judge the righteous and the wicked (3:17). This phrase repeats 3:1. God has a carefully timed plan, but we cannot know when it will be executed. Even Jesus, when He laid aside His glory in the incarnation, admitted that the Son of Man did not know the time and hour (Matt 24:36). Of course, He knows now in His exalted and glorified state! But even though he does not know the timing, Solomon trusts that God will set things right and that injustice will finally be reversed. The wicked will not ultimately get away with it (Greidanus, *Preaching Christ*, 99).

While we know God will make things right, the problem lies in that we cannot see it happening right now and we do not know when He will act. This is a tough reality for us all—stuck between confidence in belief and concern about reality. We are suspended between belief in the end times and uncertainty about what comes next (Webb, *Five Festal Garments*, 94). Meanwhile, the wicked continue to prosper, and the poor are oppressed. We live in a Psalm 73 reality where the believer is tempted toward skepticism because of the prosperity of the wicked and the suffering of the faithful, and yet like the psalmist we are called patiently to trust God and His timing! But for all of our longing and calls for justice, we have a major problem facing us, and that is what Solomon turns to next.

We Receive Death for Our Part in the Sin and Injustice of the World
ECCLESIASTES 3:18-22

Solomon shifts the discussion to the fact that, just like the band Maroon 5 says, we are like animals. Solomon says that we are like animals in that we all ultimately die. Here is his point: We want justice and we want things to be set right, but what about our part in this injustice? That is our problem. God cannot hold evil and injustice accountable without holding us accountable for our part in it. The problem is that we do not recognize our own unjust acts. When someone wrongs us—they steal our identity or break into our house—we want justice. But when we are pulled over for speeding, we want mercy (Driscoll, "Gift of Death"). We want justice for others and mercy for ourselves.

We need to recognize that even though we cry out for justice, we do not exactly want it. Are we not glad judgment day was not in 1968 (Keller, "Problem of History")? Many of us would never have existed. Are we not glad God does not set evil right immediately? None of us would be here! Solomon tells us in this section of Ecclesiastes 3 that the wages for our part in the injustice of the world is death!

We are like animals in the way we oppress one another (Murphy, *Proverbs, Ecclesiastes, Song of Songs*, 189). Solomon says God tests Adam's sons to show them they are but beasts (3:18). Later Solomon contends that God delays judgment to show we are inclined to wicked acts. He says in Ecclesiastes 8:11, "Because the sentence against a criminal act is not carried out quickly, the heart of people is filled with the desire to commit crime." God delays justice to show how wicked and beast-like we are. Thus, there is increasing wickedness, and that makes us like animals.

Animals have no concept of justice or right and wrong (Greidanus, *Preaching Christ*, 99). Contrary to the scene in *Finding Nemo*, sharks do not create societies for the humane treatment of baitfish. Yet, even though we have moral sensibilities, we treat one another like animals. We deal with one another in the most disgusting ways imaginable. From Hitler to Stalin to Polpot and the Khmer Rouge killing fields, we see barbaric acts that humans commit against other humans. My first mission trip was to Cambodia where the Khmer Rouge wiped out so much of the population. As we walked over the killing fields with the missionaries, they showed us trees where babies were bashed to death. The barbarism was sickening. That is Solomon's point. Wickedness increases, and like the days of the flood where both animals and humans died, judgment is needed!

There are echoes here in Ecclesiastes 3 to the fall of humanity in Genesis 3. Words like "Adam's sons," "beasts," and "dust" call us back to the early chapters of Genesis. God created Adam to rule over the beasts. Humanity was distinct from and superior to the beasts, but in

Genesis 3 Adam and Eve submitted to a beast—the serpent. As a result, God imposed a curse on the world. Now, in this cursed existence, we do not rule the beasts but instead are like them. There is so much chaos in this cursed world that we act like beasts. We see this reality described repeatedly throughout the Bible. The evil nations that attack Israel are called beasts (see Ps 80:13; Dan 7:3); the antichrist and the false prophet are called beasts (Rev 13). The animal kingdom is red in tooth and claw, but so is the human kingdom. Might makes right, and oppression is everywhere. The ways we treat one another are so often utterly despicable.

Solomon reveals an explicit similarity between men and beasts to show why we have no advantage over them—we both die. Each has the same "breath," which could be translated "soul" or "life." Again, this alludes to Genesis 1–3, where God breathes life into creation, but sin steals that "breath" away and brings death. Life is fleeting for animal and human alike. As Matt Chandler says, the opposable thumb is of no advantage to humans because it will decay just like the claw ("Out of Breath"). Humanity was intended to eat from the tree of life and live forever, but we all die because of sin. Death equalizes animals and humans. Death renders everything meaningless. Nothing we do matters, just as nothing animals do matters. No one writes news reports about animals when they die. And we all go to the same place. We are from the dust, and we return to the dust.

Big questions are asked in verses 21 and 22: "Who knows if the spirit of people rises upward and the spirit of animals goes downward to the earth? . . . For who can enable him to see what will happen after he dies?" The expected answer to these questions is, "No one" (Murphy, *Proverbs, Ecclesiastes, Song of Songs*, 189). Man's knowledge is truly limited to his current experience and cannot stretch beyond that. No one truly knows what happens beyond the grave because there is no way of knowing for sure. We do not know if something happens that distinguishes man and beast or that makes our actions matter more than the animals' actions.

Let us take a quick aside to explain an issue that this verse raises. This verse is not a comment on the age-old question of whether only humans have souls and animals do not, or whether animals go to heaven. I cannot see how a cat would go to heaven, but that's for another day's discussion. That is not Solomon's purpose here. He simply wants to expose the fact that we do not have certainty about what happens beyond the grave, so we are no different from animals.

However, the Bible is clear that God gives the breath of life to man and animals alike. Some like to point to Genesis 2, where God forms Adam from the dust and breathes life into him, as evidence that God gave souls to humanity but withholds that from animals, but that is simply going further than Scripture goes. The same thing said of humanity in Genesis 2:7 is also said of animals in Psalm 104:29-30. God gives the breath of life to all living creatures, and the withdrawal of that breath means death.

One major problem with contemporary Christianity is the tendency to compartmentalize soul and body (material and immaterial), so that some preachers say, "The soul is the real you—the you on the inside." But that is not biblical. The Bible shows the whole you, soul and body, is what is most important. God did not just concern Himself with the human soul and consign everything else to hell. God loves the world, including the animal kingdom. He is making all things new, including trees, dogs, and clouds. The final state of humanity is not floating bodyless on a cloud engaged in a never-ending choir practice. We are headed to a new creation where we dwell with resurrected bodies surrounded by animals, grass, and trees.

The issue Solomon addresses here is that no one knows what lies beyond death. The world is fascinated by this question, and that is why books about near-death experiences and "firsthand" accounts of what happens after death fly off bookshelves. The questions are many. Do people go to heaven and animals to nonexistence? Do all dogs go to heaven? Certainly all cats go to hell, right? Some speculate there is annihilation beyond the grave, or reincarnation, or good people go to heaven and really bad people go to hell. Solomon says no one really knows for sure. It does not matter what you think of books like *90 Minutes in Heaven* or *Heaven Is for Real*. There has never been a person who definitely died, stayed dead for several days, and then came back to life and wrote about it. That has not happened; so Solomon says, based on our limited knowledge and experience, no one can be certain about what happens after death. There is no verifiable proof; the best we can do is guess and hope.

Since we do not know what happens beyond this life, we have to rely on the eternal God who put eternity in our hearts. We are told to enjoy His gifts while we can. Ecclesiastes 3 ends with another carpe diem passage that tells us to live life to the fullest. Ecclesiastes does not deny the afterlife, but it does commend us to take death seriously. Just as the psalmist tells us to number our days (Ps 90:10-12), Ecclesiastes says that life is short and we need to make the most of it (Garrett, *Proverbs, Ecclesiastes, Song of Songs,* 305). I remember watching an episode of *Friends* a few years back where Ross was on a ride-along with a police officer. The officer made him sign a waiver that said he could not sue the city if he "scratched his knee or got his head blown off." The waiver really freaked Ross out. When a car backfired later during the ride, Ross thought someone had taken a shot at him, and when he survived, it caused him to have "a newfound respect for life." He wanted to seize every opportunity and live life to the fullest because life is a precious gift. That is kind of what Solomon is talking about. Enjoy life because it is a gift. Eat well, drink well, enjoy work, spend time with your family, and drink deeply of life!

Politics Is Meaningless
ECCLESIASTES 4:1-3,13-16; 5:8-9

Solomon begins chapter 4 by observing oppressions done under the sun and how the oppressed shed tears but no one can comfort them. People do such cruel things to one another, and no one can stop it. No one can make the oppressed feel better or set things right. Solomon expresses much angst over the situation. The reason no one can comfort the oppressed is because power is on the side of the oppressors. They can do as they please (Garrett, *Proverbs, Ecclesiastes, Song of Songs,* 305).

Therefore, politics in this fallen world is meaningless. The people elected to uphold justice, set things right, and pass laws to protect the hurting are the ones who ultimately end up doing the oppressing. The problem is that power corrupts, so even if someone sees the evil of the system and gets involved with a desire to reform things, once he has power, he is then corrupted and nothing changes (Kidner, *Ecclesiastes,* 44). In our political system, often people have to compromise their ideals in order to climb the ladder, and once they get to a position of influence they no longer are the same person anymore. Politicians, judges, and the rich can oppress the poor and the outcast who have little, if any, recourse. The powerful can do what they want to the weak, and no one can stand up for the weak, whether it is an unborn child or a slave-traded little girl. Sex traffickers pay off police to look the other way, and Liam Neeson is not flying in to save these girls. It seems hopeless.

Now one might object, "That is not true! Much can be done to help the oppressed." Yes, people can help the oppressed, but Solomon's point is that there is no net gain (Kidner, *Ecclesiastes*, 43). You cannot end oppression altogether. You might work really hard to end oppression in one little corner of the world and see a degree of success, but the oppression pops back up again in another place. The twentieth century saw Hitler overthrown, but then there was Stalin, and then there was Polpot, and now there is ISIS.

Certainly we should work for justice. We should engage in mercy ministry. This is near God's heart and talked about repeatedly throughout the Bible, especially in the wisdom literature. But without Christ, it will not be completely changed. We need to recognize that the purpose of Ecclesiastes is different from other books. While other books intend to encourage concern and help for the poor, Ecclesiastes intends to expose the meaninglessness of life in this fallen world. The whole thing is discouraging. We live in a world where it is in vogue to end injustice and put red X's on your hand. However, ours is a world where powers are corrupt, and they even use mercy for their own benefit. For example, half of the millions that have been donated to Haiti go to American companies and NGOs instead of local efforts. It ensures a culture of dependency.

This reality is so painful that the Teacher says it is better to be dead or never to have been born. The dead do not have to see what we do to one another anymore—injustice can be worse than death. Plus, those who have never been born have never had to see how we treat one another like animals under the sun. They have never seen ISIS behead or crucify children. Such chaos abounds in this cursed and broken world. Solomon is exasperated and says death seems better than life.

The Teacher returns to politics in Ecclesiastes 4:13-16 with a much-debated translation and interpretation.[6] Here is basically what is happening: A poor but wise youth supplants an old, foolish king who will not listen to counsel. Usually youth is associated with folly and age with wisdom, but not so here because the king will not listen to advice, which is the mark of foolishness (Prov 12:15). Also, Solomon's son Rehoboam was brought down as a young king because he would not listen to the

---

[6] For a good overview see Tremper Longman III, *The Book of Ecclesiastes*, NICOT (Grand Rapids: Eerdmans, 1998), 144–47.

counsel of the elders. Here in Ecclesiastes, the old king is inflexible and forgets what it was like to be young and fiery (Kidner, *Ecclesiastes*, 51–52). The youth becomes king instead. But then the youth is supplanted by a second youth, and the point is that the cycle never ends. As Duane Garrett points out, the fulfillment of political ambitions is transitory, and the praise of the masses is vapid (*Proverbs, Ecclesiastes, Song of Songs*, 308–9). The masses are fickle and flip-flop from one politician to the next. No matter how good the politician might be, nothing lasts forever. A young man may rise through the ranks and do good but become inflexible like the old king and lose the heart of the people. There is no lasting change in the political realm. They dispensed of the previous political leader, and they will dispense of you (Begg, "All Those Lonely People"). After all, Churchill was voted out of office!

Ecclesiastes 5:8-9 touches on the meaninglessness of political realities as well. It says that we should not be amazed by oppression and injustice. Again, these are difficult verses to figure out, but basically what is happening is that bureaucratic hierarchy makes oppression predictable (Murphy, *Proverbs, Ecclesiastes, Song of Songs*, 195). The bureaucracy was put in place as a safeguard of checks and balances, but instead of serving that purpose, it enables oppression by high officials, even up to the king! The citizen who wants justice can be endlessly deflected (Kidner, *Ecclesiastes*, 54–55). The idea is that government officials protect one another, so rooting out corruption is impossible (Garrett, *Proverbs, Ecclesiastes, Song of Songs*, 312). Cronyism is the inevitable result of politics. If you scratch my back, I will scratch yours. If you back this bill that I want passed, then I will make sure Nebraska gets what they want in the farm bill.

This type of bureaucratic deflection is seen in countless stories around the world. Consider the Hillsborough disaster, in which 96 people were crushed to death at a soccer match in 1989. It happened because of a poor decision by the chief superintendent—the lead police officer on the scene. And yet initially the soccer fans were blamed for the disaster because officials said too much drinking was involved. It took the victim's family members decades to clear their loved ones' names because of a bureaucratic system that covered up the police officials' poor decisions (Scraton, *Hillsborough*, XX).

Verse 9 could have two different meanings: positive or negative. The king might be for the good of the land, or the king might be taking advantage of the land. Garrett argues the king is a "necessary evil" because a community needs authority to regulate boundaries, property rights, the use of natural resources, and the like (*Proverbs, Ecclesiastes, Song of Songs*, 312). Others think the king is in on the corruption (Longman, *Ecclesiastes*, 158). Certainly Solomon was a king who violated the commands of Deuteronomy 17, which were meant to protect the people from the king. Either way this passage laments the political system in this corrupt world.

There is injustice in the world, so people are given authority to restrain evil and uphold good. The problem is that power corrupts, so those in authority often use their power for their own good and not the good of the citizens. As a result, we now completely distrust and reject authority. The way Christian people talk about the president and politicians on Facebook is absolutely sickening. The Bible commands us to pray for our leaders—believe me, you do not want to be in their position making the calls they have to make—but instead we tear them down. There is a definite tension here because absolute power corrupts, but we need authority for our own good.

Ecclesiastes Cries Out for a Better King, a Resurrection, and a Final Judgment
ECCLESIASTES 12:12-14

Solomon lays out his exasperation over leadership failures (perhaps even convicted about his own failures), death, and the lack of justice in the world. The Teacher cries out for solutions to these problems, and Jesus is the answer to each! The problem of leaders who oppress rather than make the world a better place cries out for a king who is greater than Solomon and Rehoboam and the others. Our longing for righteous political leaders who set things right is a longing for King Jesus. In His kingdom there is no oppression. There is no inequality. We see this now in seed form in the church—the outpost of the kingdom. Rich and poor, slave and free, sit down together at the table. There are no needy among us (Acts 4). We show mercy to the hurting. We get a foretaste of this in the church, but we long for the day when Jesus establishes His kingdom from sea to sea, so that all oppression is ended (see Ps 72)!

We also see the reign of death. We die and decay just like animals, and we do not know for sure what lies beyond. We fear death, and we try to push it off with diet, exercise, and cosmetic surgery, but it pursues us still. We frustratingly long for resurrection, and the New Testament reveals that for which we long. We cannot know what will happen to us after we die because no one has gone into death and come back, except for one Man (Acts 13:30). Jesus did not decay into the dust, and by faith in Him you will be raised from the dead as well. Christ's resurrection not only made it possible for us to be raised to eternal life, but it also showed us what resurrection will be like. Those who are united to Christ will live forever not as body-less souls that fly away but rather in glorified bodies where there is no pain, sorrow, or death (Rev 21:4)!

Finally, the Bible says there will be a final judgment where the wicked are raised to eternal punishment and the righteous to eternal life (Dan 12). There will be a final reckoning where all things are set right, and Ecclesiastes makes this clear as well (11:9; 12:13-14). The good news is that God brought final judgment into the middle of human history and judged sin in His Son's body on the cross. Jesus took the judgment humanity deserved at the cross, so that by repentance and faith we could be declared righteous in God's sight. He took injustice on Himself. He knows what the oppressed are going through because the greatest injustice in the history of mankind is the Son of God being murdered by evil men. Why did Christ endure that injustice? He endured injustice so that He could ultimately end injustice forever!

Conclusion

Preachers told me this narrative my entire life: all that needs to happen to change America is for us to elect the right politicians and pass the right laws. But that narrative has proven to be untrue. Building a nation on God's laws will not change America any more than it changed ancient Israel because laws do not change the human heart. Only Jesus can do that. We live in a world of oppression and injustice, and only the gospel can change things. After all, as the Christmas song reminds us, "In His Name all oppression shall cease." Even so, come quickly, King Jesus!

Reflect and Discuss

1. What do you think your purpose is in the world?
2. What ways have you sought to change the world? How have they worked?
3. What are some unjust things you see in the world?
4. What are some ways injustice rules even in America?

5. In what ways do we expect mercy for ourselves and desire justice for others?
6. What happens to us at death?
7. What should we do in light of the fact that our life on this planet is relatively short?
8. What are some ways politics encourages you?
9. What are some ways politics discourages you?
10. How can the church of Jesus Christ seek justice while waiting for Christ's return?

Religion Is Meaningless without Jesus

ECCLESIASTES 5:1-7

Main Idea: Religious ritual without the fear of God is meaningless; instead, we should approach God reverently through Christ.

I. **Religious Ritual without the Fear of God Is Meaningless (5:1-6).**
   A. Offerings (5:1)
   B. Prayers (5:2-3)
   C. Vows (5:4-6)

II. **Through Christ, We Can Approach God with Confident Reverence (5:7).**

Many Christians shared through social media a video clip of Victoria Osteen saying,

> When we obey God, we're not doing it for God . . . we're
> doing it for ourselves because God takes pleasure when we're
> happy. . . . When you come to church, when you worship Him,
> you're not doing it for God really, you're doing it for yourself.

That clip was paired with a scene from the film *Billy Madison* where a man says, "What you've just said is one of the most insanely idiotic things I have ever heard" (Blair, "Victoria Osteen"). When we hear a religious figure say out loud that we do not worship God for God, we know that is patently absurd. It is a complete reversal of the Westminster Shorter Catechism. Instead of saying that "man's chief end is to glorify God and enjoy Him forever," now contemporary Christianity seems to say that God's chief end is to glorify man and enjoy him forever.

While it is easy for us to give Mrs. Osteen a hard time, the problem is we all think this way sometimes. Our thoughts may not be as overt as Mrs. Osteen's, and we may not utter them out loud, but American Christianity has become me centered rather than God centered. We consume devotional books that are chock-full of tips on how we can have a better day but say little about the transcendent glory of God. Bible study lessons abound that act like we are the main characters of the Bible and need to become brave like David, strong in prayer like

61

Daniel, or a better father than Eli. Even preaching has become less about God and more about five ways to be a better husband, six ways to manage your money, and three tips to a godly sex life in marriage. As Mark Driscoll said, "It is possible to go to church and hear little about God and much about you" ("Guarding Your Steps"). Church has become all about us. The music and the programs are not about worshiping God or ministering to people but rather about my desires and likes. Did I like the sermon? Did he tell enough jokes? Did he stick to the Bible? Was it practical enough for my life? Was the music the kind of music I like? Was there an organ? Were there drums? Do they have a children's choir? Entire worship services are planned around the thoughts and concerns of the worshiper rather than the One being worshiped. Instead of awe, church leaders turn to gimmicks and entertainment to gain new consumers.

Worship has become all about me—my desires, my likes, my preferences, what I want—and that is nothing less than idolatry. Two men have exposed this reality with what they call cat and dog theology (Sjogren, "Cat and Dog Theology"). A dog says, "You pet me, feed me, shelter me, and love me; you must be God," but a cat says, "You pet me, feed me, shelter me, and love me; I must be God." So much modern Christianity looks just like those. God is no longer the Almighty Sovereign King of the universe; He is personal shopper, life coach, homeboy, and genie all rolled into one. We see God as a means to an end and not an end in and of Himself. We use God to get what we really want. Some come back to church, start giving money regularly, and have perfect attendance in Bible study because they hope God will take their cancer away, fix their family, provide them wealth.

I met with a man years ago who was experiencing a crisis of faith. He was 40 years old and single, and he was thinking of walking away from the church. He said he had been raised in church, had gotten away from it in early adulthood, and then came back at 35 because he desperately wanted to be married. He told me that for five years he attended worship, tithed regularly, and volunteered in ministries, and yet God had not given him a wife.

He did not want God. He wanted what God could give him. Religion has become a means to use God for what we really want rather than an experience of standing in awe of the living God. Solomon exposes that kind of religion as meaningless here in Ecclesiastes 5:1-7.

Religious Ritual without the Fear of God Is Meaningless
ECCLESIASTES 5:1-6

Throughout Ecclesiastes, Solomon has repeatedly exposed the meaninglessness of life in this cursed world. If this cursed existence under the sun is all there is, then nothing you do has meaning. Nothing you attempt to build your life on will work, and you cannot find satisfaction or meaning in pleasure or work or success or politics. But now Solomon looks beyond the sun to God and asks the question, What about religion? Can we find meaning in religion? He tells us that religion can also be a dead-end street. Why? Religion can be empty when we do not fear God. Instead, we fall into a formalism that is either rote routine or foolish attempt to manipulate God. Solomon exposes three religious rituals that are meaningless apart from faith.

Offerings (5:1)

The text starts with a command of warning: "Guard your steps when you go to the house of God" (5:1). Approach God with great caution. Why? God created man to have an intimate relationship with Him, but man's rebellions severed that relationship. Now man is separated from intimacy with God. Genesis 3 makes this clear when God casts Adam and Eve out of Eden and places cherubim outside with flaming swords to keep humanity out of paradise. Yet God still loves people and desires a relationship with them. The tabernacle, and in Solomon's day the temple—the house of God—was the place where God lived among His people to reverse what happened in Eden, if only in a small and initial way.

But still sin separates. There were specific regulations and divisions for drawing near to God in worship. After all, the cherubim show up here too. Cherubim were woven into the veil at the entrance to the most holy place where God's presence stayed (2 Chr 3:14). The most holy place in the temple symbolized a return to Eden, but sinful man had to be cautious in approaching a holy God. The divisions make this separation clear as well. Gentiles could only go so far (not a biblical restriction), women could only go so far (also not a biblical restriction), Jewish men could only go so far, and only the high priest could go into the most holy place itself, and only one time a year, and only with blood (Heb 9:25). The process of approaching God in worship and offering a sacrifice was clearly regulated in the law because it was dangerous for sinful man to come into the presence of God Almighty. Death could occur, and it did occur. So the whole sacrificial system was put in place so Holy God could live with sinful man in a reconciled relationship, but it required the shedding of blood and specific rules.

The problem was that the system put in place to allow men to approach God could be turned into formalism and legalism. The prophets repeatedly corrected the idea that the ritual itself without accompanying repentance and faith was profitable. God refuses ritual without repentance. We see a form of that correction here in Ecclesiastes. Solomon says it is better to draw near to listen than to offer the sacrifice of fools because the fool does not know that he is doing evil (5:1).

Let us begin our analysis with the negative first—the sacrifice as fools do. To what does this refer? It refers to formalism and manipulation. The sacrifice of fools is a formalism that performs the ritual in order to gain God's favor, when the heart of the worshiper is actually far from God. No faith in or fear of God accompanies the ritual. Fools believe the sacrifice will automatically cancel out their sin without the need to repent (Greidanus, *Preaching Christ*, 131). Or the worshiper was simply going through the motions because "this is just what you do if you are an Israelite." Religious form without spiritual substance is the notion. This too repulses God.

We do the same thing. We can fall into the rut of just going through the motions because "that's just what we do." We do religious things, but our heart is not in it. It is possible for people to show up for worship week after week, year after year, and decade after decade, but their lives not really be changed. They are still cruel to others, harsh to their spouses, perverted in their jokes, and indifferent toward their children, as they have always been.

Not only can we fall into the rut; we can also adopt the mind-set that our religious rituals will somehow gain us God's favor. We can offer something to God like money, our service, or our attendance at religious events because we think it will cause God to give us what we want. This is an attempt at manipulation. I remember talking to a guy who had just started coming back to church and bringing his family. He told me that the reason he did was because he was having financial struggles and had an invention patent pending, and he was thinking that if he got his family back in church then God would bless him with his patent being approved and his invention becoming a huge success.

We can all fall victim to this way of thinking. And this way of thinking is even reinforced sometimes by our revival and crusade testimonies. At these huge revival meetings popular celebrities and successful athletes get up and tell about how when they started walking with Jesus, the Lord blessed them and gave them all of this success. We come away with the idea that if I just start tithing, then I will become rich like that person. That is a form of paganism or magic where you perform rituals for God so that He will give you what you really want in return. God is a means not an end in this scenario. That is not the gospel. That is not authentic Christianity. As Mark Driscoll said, "Just because you go to church and worship God does not mean you are not a fool" ("Guarding Your Steps"). What is so bad is that the fool is ignorant that he is doing wrong, angering God, and adding to the separation. He is not helping a thing. He may actually be making things worse.

God, through His prophets, repeatedly criticizes this mind-set. In 1 Samuel 15:22 Samuel says,

> Does the LORD take pleasure in burnt offerings and sacrifices as much as in obeying the LORD? Look: to obey is better than sacrifice, to pay attention is better than the fat of rams.

The word *obey* in that verse can be translated "listen," and the idea is listening with the result that you obey what God says. That leads to the first part of what Solomon said in Ecclesiastes 5. The key to worship is listening to and obeying God. Part of the sacrificial process was the priest reading from God's law and explaining it as an accompaniment to the sacrifice (Greidanus, *Preaching Christ*, 131). Revelation is the key to Christian worship. The God of the universe wants us to worship Him for who He is and what He has done, and He has revealed that to us in the Bible.

Unfortunately, we often reduce worship to merely singing, but worship is all of life (Rom 12:1-2). Worship has to do with whether you obey the revealed will of God laid out in the Bible. You can come to as many worship gatherings as you want and raise your hands high in the air, but if you cannot obey God's Word, then you have a worship problem. The Bible authoritatively tells us what to do with our time, our money, our families, our sex lives, and so much more, and we are called to submit to it. The problem is that instead of listening and submitting, we tell the Word what we will obey. We find it easy to submit to the parts we like and agree with, but we conveniently find alternative interpretations for the things we do not like. "Well, that's not what that verse actually means." "Well, my situation is different." "Well, that is not how I interpret the text." Later in this passage Solomon talks about optional promises (i.e., vows) that we make to God and that we must keep.

It reminds me of a friend in high school who was sleeping with his girlfriend, and when I confronted him about it, he said, "I never made that promise to God. I never promised to save myself for marriage." Well, it does not matter whether you promised that; it is right there in the Bible. It is not a negotiable situation. It is not up for debate or a vote. God has revealed Himself to us in the Word, so we must listen and obey. That is why we spend so much time on the sermon in our worship gatherings. That is why preaching rather than singing is central to our worship gatherings. We are here mainly to listen to God, not to talk or sing back to Him. Why? Because, when the Word is rightly preached, our God is speaking from heaven, and He is speaking to us. So we must draw near to Him and listen to Him.

Prayers (5:2-3)

Solomon moves to the topic of prayer (Longman, *Ecclesiastes*, 151). He says not to be hasty with your mouth or with words in your heart before God. He is speaking of both verbal and internal dialogue with God, which has to do with prayer. He commands us to be reserved with our words in our prayer lives because of God's awesomeness in heaven in contrast with our sinful frailty here on earth. He is the judge and king of the universe, so address Him with respect and restraint.

Part of the problem here again is an attempt to manipulate God. People think if they just pile up word after word after word, then God will hear and answer their prayers. Jesus warns about the exact same situation when He says,

> When you pray, don't babble like the idolaters, since they imagine they'll be heard for their many words. Don't be like them, because your Father knows the things you need before you ask Him. (Matt 6:7-8)

The presumption is that one can be in a position of control (Garrett, *Proverbs, Ecclesiastes, Song of Songs*, 311). The person thinks because of how they pray, what they pray, or how many words they use that God will be favorable toward them. Some people think they must pray in King James language for God to actually listen and answer. Others think they have to be casual and refer to God as "Daddy" to be heard. What you say or how you say it is not the issue. The issue is your heart. But we so often think our heavenly Father is like earthly parents who can be asked at the right time or in the right way and we can get the answer we want.

Our children learn this. One Saturday my daughter Emma wanted a chocolate cupcake, but instead of coming up to us and asking, "Can I have a cupcake?" to which we probably would have replied, "No, you will ruin your dinner," she asked, "Do you think I ought to taste test that chocolate cupcake to make sure I like it before you pack it in my lunch Monday?" After we laughed, we said, "Sure. You can have the cupcake." The problem is that we think God can be manipulated like that. The answer to your prayer does not depend on what you say, how you ask it, how many words you use, or even the formality or casualness of your words. Rather, it depends on a heavenly Father who knows what is best for you. We have nothing to barter with or to offer God. We just ask with humble hearts, and we trust that how He answers is best.

Solomon says the reason to be reserved in prayer is because dreams come from much work and "a fool's voice from many words" (5:3). Proverbs is clear that fools speak a lot and love the sound of their own voices, but what is the connection here with the dream? Much work makes one tired, which leads to sleep and dreams, but dreams are not real. Thus, you are living in a fantasy world if you think your many words will affect God (Longman, *Ecclesiastes*, 152). Instead, come like the tax collector who beats his chest in Jesus's parable and says, "God be merciful to me a sinner" (Luke 18:13-14) (Eswine, *Recovering Eden*, 151). Just like our children, when they are hurting, do not have to wrangle us for us to bend down and help them, neither do we have to wrangle our heavenly Father. He knows the things we need before we ask Him.

Vows (5:4-6)

Solomon now turns his attention to vows. He says, "When you make a vow . . . don't delay fulfilling it," because God "does not delight in fools." Vows were pledges worshipers would make to God as part of the offering or sacrifice process. The vow was made so that God might answer a specific request. Deuteronomy 12:11 states,

> then Yahweh your God will choose the place to have His name dwell. Bring there everything I command you: your burnt offerings, sacrifices, offerings of the tenth, personal contributions, and all your choice offerings you vow to the LORD.

Deuteronomy 23:21-23 adds,

> *If you make a vow to the LORD your God, do not be slow to keep it,*
> *because He will require it of you, and it will be counted against*
> *you as sin. But if you refrain from making a vow, it will not be*
> *counted against you as sin. Be careful to do whatever comes from*
> *your lips, because you have freely vowed what you promised to the*
> *LORD your God.*

Look at one clear example of how vows worked. Numbers 21:2-3 says,

> *Then Israel made a vow to the LORD, "If You will deliver this people*
> *into our hands, we will completely destroy their cities." The LORD*
> *listened to Israel's request, the Canaanites were defeated, and Israel*
> *completely destroyed them and their cities. So they named the place*
> *Hormah.*

So vows were made to gain God's favor in order to urge God to grant a specific request. The worshiper could offer God a sacrifice, money, or property in exchange for God meeting the request. Thus, it was a kind of "I will do this for You if You do this for me." Another example is barren Hannah, who asked the Lord for a child and vowed that he would be a Nazarite. When she weaned Samuel, she took him to serve at the tabernacle with Eli (1 Sam 1).

Even today during a crisis people often make vows or promises to God. "God, if You will come through for me, then I promise I will do this for You in return." If God will take away the cancer, get you a job, give you a spouse, or get your children out of a jam, then you promise to walk more closely with God. The danger today, as it was back then, is that once the crisis is over, the vow might go unfulfilled. Now you want to hold on to that costly thing you promised or wait on doing what you vowed, and that delay angers God.

This reality can happen to all of us. I remember reading a book titled *I Told Me So*, in which the author talked about self-deception and how one of the ways we deceive ourselves is through procrastination. We say we will do something, but we do not do it immediately, and then ultimately we fail to do it at all. The author talked about sitting in a worship service looking at a commitment card for a mission endeavor his church was doing, and he thought to himself that there was only one week left to turn in the money he had committed. He determined in his heart to write the check as soon as he got home. He put the commitment card in his Bible, and a year later when he opened up to that same passage, he again saw the card and realized that he had forgotten to give to the mission cause (Elshof, *I Told Me So*, 43–45). People can get caught up in a moment of enthusiasm or crisis, and in that moment they make a promise to God or some kind of vow. You can hear a sermon and be convicted, and inside you say, "Yes, I need that. I need community. I need to confess my adultery. I need to get rid of my hidden sin so I can be free of it" (Chandler, "Approaching the Divine"). You leave the service with the best of intentions, but you never follow through on them.

Solomon says in verse 5 that it is better not to make a vow than to vow and not pay it. Hold your tongue. Keep your mouth shut. One example in our culture where we make vows is marriage. It is better to be single and unmarried than to get married and break your vows. In addition to marriage vows, we make private and public promises to God—like dedicating ourselves that we will raise our children to know and love Jesus, that we will be a better spouse, that we will give to some church campaign, or that we will not lose our temper anymore with our children—but we fail to keep our promises. We dedicate ourselves in front of God and the church to raise our babies right, and we start out so well, but once they grow up and ball games or recitals start happening on Sundays, we get out of church. You make a promise not to yell at your kids on Sunday, but by Wednesday you are tired, and they grate on your nerves so you explode.

Solomon says not to let your mouth make you sin and not to tell the messenger it was a mistake to make that vow. The *messenger* most likely refers to a temple official who ensured vows were fulfilled (Enns, *Ecclesiastes*, 68). So when worshipers would make a public vow at the temple, the messenger would go to the houses of people who had delayed in keeping their vows and point out their failures.

So your mouth dragged you into the sin of making a vow you could not keep, but do not try to excuse yourself by saying it was a mistake (Longman, *Ecclesiastes*, 154). That will anger God all the more. The words you voice to God matter to God. He hears them all! People do this type of thing with their vows all the time. Again, they do it with marriage. "We were in sin and should not have gotten married. This is not a godly marriage, so we need to end it." People do it with other vows and promises to God, and this leads God to destroy the works of their hands (5:6; a major concern throughout Ecclesiastes). Do not try to excuse yourself; instead own it and confess it.

Do not try to hide it either. The story in Acts about Ananias and Sapphira illustrates this (Acts 5). They sold some property and said they were giving all of the proceeds to the church, but they secretly kept back some for themselves, and God killed both of them. It would have been OK for them to keep some of the money; they just should have been honest about it.

Solomon exposes throughout this section the meaninglessness of religion that tries to manipulate God. The idea is, "I'll do this ritual for You if You will come through and do this for me." So much of American "Christianity" is this same kind of paganism. We try to bargain with God to get what we want. We think if we do what God wants, then He will do what we want. I even see this in church signs that say things like, "God blessed America because America blessed God." Do what God wants, and then He will do what you want. That is idolatry or sorcery. That is not the gospel!

Through Christ, We Can Approach God with Confident Reverence
ECCLESIASTES 5:7

The author concludes the passage by again mentioning the fantasy of thinking our words affect God, and then He calls us to fear God. We have a hard time understanding the concept of the fear of the Lord because we live in a culture that has no reverence for authority. We no longer approach parents, teachers, or coaches with respect. Lack of respect and honor has bled over into a new casual Christianity where Jesus is our homeboy or copilot and not so much our absolute, formidable King and awe-inspiring, sovereign Master.

We should humbly submit to and stand in awe of God who knows all of our sins and empty promises. People may try to object to this idea and say, "Well, that is just the Old Testament," but Jesus warns us to fear Him who can destroy soul and body in hell (Matt 10:28). We are called to reverent awe of God.

The only way we can appropriately approach God is through Jesus. We are separated from God because of our sin, and the temple system gave specific regulations for approaching God. However, that system was temporary because it could never once-for-all cleanse the worshiper and reconcile him with God. But Jesus is the better priest and the better sacrifice who can cleanse and reconcile us for all time! When He died on the cross—not only for all of our sins but also for all of our empty religion and promises—what happened? The veil separating man from God's presence was torn in two from top to bottom, showing that man once again had access to Holy God (Matt 27:51). No longer was the way to paradise blocked. Now we can come with both confidence and awe before the living God. Hebrews 10 makes this so clear:

> *Therefore, as He was coming into the world, He said:*
>
> *You did not want sacrifice and offering, but You prepared a body for Me. You did not delight in whole burnt offerings and sin offerings. Then I said, "See—it is written about Me in the volume of the scroll—I have come to do Your will, God!"*
>
> *After He says above, You did not want or delight in sacrifices and offerings, whole burnt offerings and sin offerings (which are offered according to the law), He then says, See, I have come to do Your will. He takes away the first to establish the second. By this will of God, we have been sanctified through the offering of the body of Jesus Christ once and for all.*
>
> *Every priest stands day after day ministering and offering the same sacrifices time after time, which can never take away sins. But this man, after offering one sacrifice for sins forever, sat down at the right hand of God. He is now waiting until His enemies are made His footstool. For by one offering He has perfected forever those who are sanctified. . . .*
>
> *Therefore, brothers, since we have boldness to enter the sanctuary through the blood of Jesus, by a new and living way He has opened for us through the curtain (that is, His flesh), and since we have a great high priest over the house of God, let us draw near with a true heart in full assurance of faith, our hearts sprinkled clean from an evil conscience and our bodies washed in pure water. Let us hold on to the confession of our hope without wavering, for He who promised is faithful.* (Heb 10:5-14,19-23)

Hebrews 10 recalls the critique of the sacrificial system. The sacrifices did not automatically cancel sin. They needed to be accompanied by obedience, and even then they could not deal with sin permanently. They had to be repeated again and again. Hebrews explains that Jesus fulfilled both the requirement of obedience because He did God's will (10:8-9) and the requirement of a better sacrifice because His dealt with sin once for all time (10:12). Therefore, we can boldly enter the sanctuary (10:19).

Despite our careless words and empty religion, Jesus brings us back to God. He fully cleanses us and allows us to come boldly before God's throne. We do this individually in prayer and private worship. Jesus makes this clear in John 4 with the woman at the well. You no longer have to go to a specific physical location to worship God. You can pray and worship Him anywhere. But while we can approach God in private worship, we approach Him in a special way in corporate worship. Now, according to Ephesians 2, we are the new temple where God dwells. Hebrews 12 says that when we gather for corporate worship, we gather at Mount Zion in the presence of God Almighty, innumerable angels, and the saints who have passed on. But we are still called to listen and fear! Hebrews 12 states,

> Make sure that you do not reject the One who speaks. For if they did not escape when they rejected Him who warned them on earth, even less will we if we turn away from Him who warns us from heaven. . . . Therefore, since we are receiving a kingdom that cannot be shaken, let us hold on to grace. By it, we may serve God acceptably, with reverence and awe, for our God is a consuming fire. (Heb 12:25,28-29)

We draw near to God's presence in corporate worship to listen to God and to make an offering with reverence and awe. But now we do not offer animals; we offer our bodies! Romans 12:1 says, "Therefore, brothers, by the mercies of God, I urge you to present your bodies as a living sacrifice, holy and pleasing to God; this is your spiritual worship."

Conclusion

Christ has changed how we approach God, and He has revitalized our religious rituals. Now in Christ we can boldly approach the throne of grace to pray anywhere and anytime, and our Father hears us for Christ's sake. We do not have to take off work, spend lots of money on a plane ticket, fly to Israel, and walk into a physical structure to draw near to God (Driscoll, "Guarding Your Steps"). We can come anytime we want, privately.

Now there are no sacred structures, but there is a sacred people that gathers together. As Alistair Begg argues, there is nothing special about the buildings we worship in except that God's people are there ("Concerning Worship"). When we gather corporately at Mount Zion, we listen to God's Word, we sing of His glory, and we offer our lives to Him. All that we are is offered as worship to our God: our bodies, our money, our praise, our confession, our love of our brothers, and so much more.

And now, in Christ, we let our yes be yes and our no be no (Matt 5:37). We keep our word and make good on our promises. How glorious would it be if the church of the Lord Jesus Christ was the one place in all the earth where people kept their vows and made good on their promises?! If that is not true of us, then we need to repent and confess. Let us stand in awe of our great God through the grace of Jesus Christ, and let us offer our whole lives and all of our words as pleasing sacrifices to Him!

Reflect and Discuss

1. What are some ways we have made worship all about us? How are the dog and the cat both wrong?
2. Certainly man-centered worship appeals to our ego, but what might be some other reasons we resonate with it?
3. Why do you think awe at God's magnificent transcendence has been replaced in our culture with Jesus as our homeboy?
4. What are some ways we try to manipulate God to do what we want?
5. Have you ever gotten into a rut in your religious rituals? What did you do to get out?
6. If worship is more than singing, what does it look like to worship God and bring Him glory whether we eat or drink, or whatever we do (1 Cor 10:31)?
7. How can you pray without attempting to manipulate God?
8. In what kinds of situations do you usually bargain with God? How has that worked?
9. Why do we procrastinate on fulfilling promises we make to God? How can we fight against this?
10. How should the fact that you have free access to God revolutionize your worship life?

Money Is Meaningless without Jesus

ECCLESIASTES 4:7-12 AND 5:10–6:12

Main Idea: Instead of trying to find satisfaction in money and possessions, find it in Jesus and His gifts.

I. **Pursuing Satisfaction in Money Is Meaningless.**
   - A. You'll never have enough (5:10).
   - B. You'll attract leeches (5:11).
   - C. You'll not sleep well (5:12).
   - D. You'll hurt yourself (5:13).
   - E. You'll never be truly secure (5:14).
   - F. You'll leave it behind (5:15-16).
   - G. You'll be a miserable person (5:17).

II. **Antidotes to Satisfaction in Money**
   - A. Meaningful relationships (4:7-12)
   - B. Contentment and joy in what God has given you (5:18–6:9)
   - C. Jesus (6:10-12)

Disney showed a short film in theaters before *Big Hero 6* (2014) called *The Feast*. The story is told entirely through the eyes of a dog. In the beginning he is homeless and scrounging through trash desperate to find food, when a man finds him and takes him home. He is so happy to have a meal that he devours a bowl of dog food. The man begins to feed the dog table scraps like bacon, eggs, and ice cream, to the point that the pup becomes dissatisfied with regular dog food. Then the man falls in love with a woman, and they begin to eat healthy and feed the dog only dog food. The dog loved the scraps and no longer wants just dog food. But when the man and the woman break up, the man begins to gorge himself on junk food that he also feeds to the dog. Despite that he now has the food he loves, the dog knows that his owner is miserable. He orchestrates a reunion with the ex-girlfriend, and eventually the couple gets married. Now, the dog loves living in a happy home where he contentedly eats his bowl of dog food.

We resonate with that story, and our hearts say, "Yes! Contentment with what you have and having people to enjoy life with is better than having a lot of stuff!" The Bible agrees with this sentiment and offers much wisdom on the topic. Proverbs 15:16-17 says, "Better a little with the fear of the LORD than great treasure with turmoil. Better a meal of vegetables where there is love than a fattened ox with hatred." So a modest meal in a loving family is better than a filet mignon eaten in solitude. Solomon says something similar in Ecclesiastes 4:6: "Better one handful with rest than two handfuls with effort and a pursuit of the wind." The argument is that one handful of money, possessions, and food is better than two handfuls of that stuff when you are not satisfied and are chasing the wind. Better is a little when you enjoy what you have with the family you have than having a bunch of stuff with no one with whom to enjoy it!

The problem is that while our hearts resonate with a story about joy in contentment, our hearts are also prone to gravitate away from that compelling story toward discontentment. Even in the short movie, the dog starts out homeless and longs for any food. He was once grateful for just a bowl of dog food, but he becomes dissatisfied with it. The same is true for us. Our hearts begin to think that to be truly happy we need more than we have right now. This is a problem regardless of our financial station. The pull for more than we have is strong. No matter what our tax bracket, we think more is the answer.

I have a friend who is an extremely wealthy and generous Christian, but he once wrote this on Facebook: "I must be missing something. I was just reading an article that is speculating that Romney will run in 2016 and a remark was made that the wealthy, making $200,000 per year, will get all the tax breaks. First of all, $200,000 per year is not rich . . ." What? $200,000 isn't rich? Most of us read that statement and think he is ridiculous for making it, but we have the same mind-set. We think that whatever we have is not enough—whatever we have is not wealthy. And yet millions of people in the world, if not billions, would kill to have what we have right now and we take for granted! Our hearts are fickle and pull us away from contentment to the craving for more and more and more. In Ecclesiastes 4:7-12 and 5:10–6:12, Solomon exposes the foolishness of seeking meaning and satisfaction in money, and instead he calls us to contentment and joy in what we have (Phil 4:11-13)!

Pursuing Satisfaction in Money Is Meaningless

Solomon has made the point all along in Ecclesiastes that if this cursed world is all there is, then everything is meaningless. It does not matter how much pleasure, success, or stuff you have, you come away empty. Solomon's purpose is to expose the foolishness of life without God and to show us, through the Spirit, that everything is meaningless without Messiah Jesus.

He has already shown us that money and possessions will not bring meaning and satisfaction to life. Solomon knows this full well—better than most. After all, he had more money and stuff than anyone ever had before him. Previously in Ecclesiastes, Solomon condemned both extremes when it comes to money (4:4-7). He condemned the lazy man as a fool, and he condemned the workaholic because working hard to earn more money will not satisfy. Instead, he called us to contentment and joy in what we have. Here in the middle of Ecclesiastes 5, he takes up this topic again in more detail. His main point is to show that the idea that money and possessions bring meaning and satisfaction to life is absurd (Enns, *Ecclesiastes*, 71). In fact, he bookends this passage on wealth with the keyword *hevel* ("futile") to show that pursuing satisfaction in money is meaningless, and he gives seven reasons this is the case.

You'll Never Have Enough (5:10)

Those who love money will never be satisfied by money, and Solomon calls this kind of discontentment "futile." Solomon's statement has nothing to do with tax bracket; he does not mention an amount. His statement has everything to do with the heart. You can love money and have a lot, and you can love money and have a little. The issue is not how much you have; the issue is the heart. The issue is failure to be content with what you have. There was a time in your life when you would have jumped at the opportunity to have the income, family, and house that you presently have, but now it is not enough.

The sinfulness of the human heart causes us to see what we have right now as not enough. You can see this reality in the people who win a jackpot in Vegas and go right back to the same slot machine to get more (Begg, "In Search of Meaning"). A reporter once asked Rockefeller, who was the richest man in the world, "Which million that you have earned was your favorite?" And Rockefeller answered, "My next million" (Begg, "In Search of Meaning"). Nothing is ever good enough. Solomon's point is difficult for most of us to believe because we think if we had more money we would be the exception, and we would be satisfied with what we had. But our own experience tells us that is not true—after all, there was a time in our lives when we would have thought what we earn right now is a lot of money. We thought we would be content. Satisfied. But we amaze our friends and surprise ourselves to discover that we are not content.

We can see from the time we were children and on into adulthood the thing we thought would make us truly happy never really did. When I was a child and had a Nintendo, I desperately wanted the *WrestleMania* Nintendo game. I asked my parents to get it for me for Christmas. I thought that was all I needed to be happy. I was so excited to get it that I woke up at 4:00 a.m. before my parents or any of my brothers on Christmas day and ran downstairs. I found the wrapped gift that looked like a Nintendo game, and I ripped it open, revealing *WrestleMania*. I plugged it into the game system and started to play. By the time my parents woke a few hours later, I was bored of *WrestleMania*!

We are not naturally content with what we have (Driscoll, "Redefining Riches"). We are always looking to the next thing. Solomon's point is that since you will never have enough, it is not worth making the pursuit of money and possessions your life's goal!

You'll Attract Leeches (5:11)

Like the rapper Notorious B.I.G., Solomon says that money creates all kinds of problems. Solomon says the more money you make, the more leeches will want a piece of what you have, and ultimately you will watch it go away. The person who has wealth does not really get to enjoy the fruits of what he has earned (Longman, *Ecclesiastes*, 165). Creditors, family, "friends," the IRS, and more will consume what you have. Everyone will have a hand out to get what you got.

One tragic story that shows the truth of this statement involves Bernie Kosar, who used to be a star quarterback in the NFL. Kosar made tens of millions of dollars in his playing career. And he also made at least that much, if not more, as a businessman after his playing days. And yet he had to file for bankruptcy. A reporter asked him about this, and he revealed that there was a time in his life when he was paying 60 cell phone plans. He told the reporter that he only used one cell phone, but he was paying for 60 plans (Brennan, "Athletes"). In addition to this, an ex-wife, attorneys, the IRS, former teammates who needed thousands to get out of debt, the economic recession, and foolish financial advisors mooched millions off of him. Now we might think we would be different if we had as much money as he had, but Solomon says we are kidding ourselves!

You'll Not Sleep Well (5:12)

The author says the common worker will sleep well regardless of how much he has because he is content with what he has. His work tires him, it gives him what he needs, and it gives him good rest. In contrast, the wealth of the rich will not allow them to sleep. The rich person's appetite for more and more never allows them to rest or to enjoy what they have. They constantly think about the next business deal or the leeches that will take from them, they fret about an investment that might go bad, or they lie awake worrying about a recession (Greidanus, *Preaching Christ*, 150). Worry and anxiety are their actual rewards.

I remember watching a YouTube video of a motivational speaker who wanted to teach young people how to become successful and rich, and he gave them the examples of stars like Beyoncé and 50 Cent. He said these stars would go days without sleeping and they would miss meals just to capitalize on the moment. Their motto was that you can sleep when you are dead! That is the reason the wealthy cannot sleep; they keep worrying about the next venture. However, those who are not rich but still love money also run into the problem of restlessness. They lie awake at night thinking and worrying about money. Solomon warns us in this verse that money does not bring peace, rest, or enjoyment to life!

You'll Hurt Yourself (5:13)

The author says there is a sickening evil under the sun, which calls us back to the curse of Genesis 3. Part of the brokenness of this world is that riches held back by their owner hurt him! Hoarding riches does not help you; it hurts you. Being stingy with what you have can destroy your family because of your workaholism, it can ruin your health because you do not sleep well, and it can harm your character. An interesting article, written by a non-Christian, called "What Wealth Does to Your Soul," argues that making lots of money makes you selfish, unhappy, and dishonest (Lewis). The article cites studies that revealed the richer people are the more likely they are to cut off other drivers, not give pedestrians the right of way, and take candy from children. Sounds like Ebenezer Scrooge to me! The Bible is clear that the joyful life is the generous life, not the stingy, selfish life.

You'll Never Be Truly Secure (5:14)

Ecclesiastes 5:14 describes a man who loses his wealth in a bad venture. It does not tell us the exact nature of the bad venture. Perhaps an economic recession hits the man hard. We had some friends who were wealthy and generous, and they lost almost everything in the real estate collapse and economic recession. Others lose their fortunes in a bad business move, pyramid schemes, gambling, or with a posse like so many athletes have. In fact, statistics say that within two years of leaving professional football, 78 percent of players are bankrupt or are in financial distress (Torre, "How [and Why]").

The problem is that the man in Ecclesiastes 5:14 has a family to provide for, and yet he has nothing to give or leave to his family. Even if he did, Solomon has already depressingly stated that leaving a legacy will not work because your family will probably squander it (2:18-19). He was right. Statistics tell us that "60% of families waste away their wealth by the end of the second generation. By the end of the third generation, 90% of families have little or nothing left of money received from grandparents" (Voorhees, "Why Most Families Lose Their Wealth"). Thus, Solomon argues that wealth is an insecure basis for happiness (Garrett, *Proverbs, Ecclesiastes, and Song of Songs*, 314). After all, Proverbs said that wealth sprouts wings and flies away (Prov 23:4-5), which leads to the next reason.

You'll Leave It Behind (5:15-16)

Ecclesiastes 5:15-16 echoes creation and the curse of Genesis 3. We brought nothing into this world, and we will lose everything when we die. After all, Ecclesiastes has made it abundantly clear that we return to the dust. The point is that if we do not lose our money in a bad business deal, then we will certainly lose it at death. Thus, we lose it one way or the other. We enter this world naked, with nothing in our hands. Every parent knows this is true. Babies do not come out of their momma's stomach holding the cash necessary to pay the hospital bills. And we die the same way—with nothing. Paul says the same thing in 1 Timothy 6:6, and a country song called "Trailer Hitch" makes the same point. You never see a hearse with a trailer hitch, so why spend all this effort to make so much money when death will cancel all of our work and earnings? Jesus asks us why we would kill ourselves to make as much money and accumulate as much stuff as possible when we will lose it all in the end anyway. He calls that foolishness in Luke 12. Steve Jobs (1955–2011) had a net worth of $10.2 billion when he died. We all know how much he took with him. Not a penny.

You'll Be a Miserable Person (5:17)

Solomon's final point is that the rich man eats in darkness with much sorrow, sickness, and anger. This man does not enjoy life. He is lonely and has no one with whom to share his wealth. Thus, trying to find satisfaction in money and stuff is meaningless. It never truly brings satisfaction, and then you die. This point is illustrated in the poignant story by Tolstoy called, "How Much Land Does a Man Need?" The story is about a content peasant farmer who says that he needs just a little land to be happy. The Devil overhears the man and commits to getting him more land in an effort to destroy him. The peasant farmer gets a little land but is not satisfied, so he trades it for more land but is not satisfied. This goes on repeatedly till the man dies in his quest for a huge chunk of land, and the story ends with the servant burying him and this telling statement: "Six feet from his head to his heels was all he needed." Death is the great equalizer! It cancels out all the earnings we have! Why kill yourself to gain more money, more stuff, and more land, when you are just going to be shoved into a hole in the ground at the end and eaten by worms?!

Antidotes to Satisfaction in Money

Meaningful Relationships (4:7-12)

The author writes this:

> Again, I saw futility under the sun: There is a person without a companion, without even a son or brother, and though there is no end to all his struggles, his eyes are still not content with riches. "So who am I struggling for," he asks, "and depriving myself from good?" This too is futile and a miserable task.
>
> Two are better than one because they have a good reward for their efforts. For if either falls, his companion can lift him up; but pity the one who falls without another to lift him up. Also, if two lie down together, they can keep warm; but how can one person alone keep warm? And if someone overpowers one person, two can resist him. A cord of three strands is not easily broken.

The point is simple: we are made for community and meaningful relationships. Why kill yourself trying to make so much money when you

have no one with whom to share it? Meaningful relationships bring
more joy than any amount of money ever could. When you are blessed,
there is greater joy in sharing that blessing with another. If you stumble
and fall, a companion who can lift you up and even save your life is
invaluable. A cold winter night and its chill can be overcome by the
embrace of your mate. Someone attacks you who is stronger than you?
Well, wait until you and your beast of a friend gets hold of him! You
struggle to win the battles of life going it alone? A friend on either side
will give you the strength to endure and succeed. Of course no three-
cord strand is superior to our Triune God! Never forget. Jesus who was
sent by the Father and empowered by the Holy Spirit died for a church,
not just individual souls. We were created and redeemed for community, a community beautifully displayed in our Triune God.

Contentment and Joy in What God Has Given You (5:18–6:9)

Solomon follows his condemnation of the love of money with another
carpe diem passage. He calls us to contentment during our short life.
The key is not how much or how little you have but rather how you
view what you do have. The basic idea is to enjoy what God has given
you instead of craving more, more, and more. Enjoy food, enjoy drink,
enjoy your work, and enjoy your spouse and your family because until
you enjoy what you already have, new things will not help or satisfy. Why
should God provide more for you if you are not content with what He
has already given you (Driscoll, "Redefining Riches")? You can be so
concerned about what you do not have that you fail to enjoy and show
gratitude for what you do have!

The end of chapter 5 and the beginning of chapter 6 explain that
what you have, where you are in life, and the ability to enjoy those things
are all from God. It is not just what you have that is a gift from God; the
ability to enjoy it is also a gift. To be able rightly and fully to enjoy the
things of this world is a gift of God's grace (Garrett, *Proverbs, Ecclesiastes,
Song of Songs*, 315). God gives this ability so that you do not remember
the misery of this cursed world because time flies when you are having
fun. The key factor to all of this is God. One can only enjoy material
blessings as rightly intended and designed in dependence on God.

Chapter 6 begins, echoing the curse with the language of "sickening tragedy," by presenting a man who has everything the world says
you need to be truly happy (interestingly, the very things promised to
Solomon in 2 Chr 1:12). But God does not give him the ability to enjoy

what he has. What makes this situation more awful is that someone else will enjoy that for which the man worked so hard (cf. Eccl 2:18-23). Thus, a man can live the American dream but find it is actually a nightmare!

What should we make of God's sovereign choice mentioned here? God sovereignly allots things to us, and He even allots the ability or inability to enjoy what He has given to us. God chose what you would get and where you would be stationed in life. He chose the life, family, job, skills, looks, and intellect you have. But why in the world would God give someone something but withhold the ability to enjoy it? Because He knows what is best for us. He gives some the inability to enjoy what they have because in His goodness He will not give you something that drives you away from Him. He knows there is no such thing as happiness apart from Him.

Jesus teaches His disciples that it is hard for a rich man to enter the kingdom of heaven—so hard that it takes a miraculous work of Almighty God (Greidanus, *Preaching Christ*, 144). Perhaps one way He saves the rich is by the meaninglessness of riches that cannot be enjoyed. When you get to the top and get everything you ever wanted but still feel empty inside, then you know that there must be something better and more satisfying out there. God wants to expose our need of Him and show us that riches cannot be ultimate. Disallowing the ability to find satisfaction in stuff is God's goodness to us because nothing but God can ultimately satisfy!

Ecclesiastes 6:3-6 shows that a man can have the blessed life of the Old Testament—wealth, kids, and long life—yet not be satisfied. If you cannot enjoy life, then a stillborn baby is better off (6:3). Why? Because the rich man is all alone. He does not get a proper burial (6:3), which means he is unlamented and no one misses him (Hunt, *Ecclesiastes*, 28). People might be at your funeral to fight over your money, but they do not shed tears of sorrow for you. People will deeply grieve over a miscarried baby but not this man. And the stillborn baby at least gets to rest like the laborer in chapter 5, and the baby does not know the pain of this world. On the other hand, this man experiences the misery of no rest or satisfaction. Again, death is the great equalizer that makes all of the wealthy man's accomplishments as null as a miscarried child who did nothing and had nothing.

All the work a man does is for his mouth, but his appetite is not satisfied (6:7). Life is a treadmill; we work so that we can eat so that we can have the strength to work so that we can eat (Kidner, *Ecclesiastes*, 61). We have uncontrolled appetites to consume food, money, technology, and so much more, but the problem is the "more" we get is never enough because the human heart was made to be satisfied only in God alone. Thus, no amount of money or things will ever fill our void (Hunt, *Ecclesiastes*, 22). Interestingly, the wise really have no advantage over fools, and the poor wise man cannot get a leg up either (6:8). The problem of dissatisfied appetites affects every station of life, and even if the poor man figured out how to make his way in the world and get some success, he would be as unsatisfied as the rich man. Therefore, Solomon concludes that the sight of the eyes is better than the roving appetite, and he writes "futile" over the whole section (6:9). It is better to be content with what you have—what is right in front of your eyes—than constantly crave more!

All of this misery is to expose our need for God and drive us to contentment in Him (Kidner, *Ecclesiastes*, 60). That money and things are fleeting and fail to ultimately satisfy reveals our need for God and shows that everything is meaningless without Jesus, who is the final antidote to materialism. "I am satisfied with Jesus" has always been the song God desires to be the theme of the human heart. This is the focus of our final section.

Jesus (6:10-12)

Duane Garrett helpfully points out that the final verses of Ecclesiastes 6 are a reflection on the early chapters of Genesis and the fall of mankind (*Proverbs, Ecclesiastes, Song of Songs*, 317–18). It repeatedly references Adam and even the naming of things (6:10; cf. Gen 2:19). It is known what man is, and Ecclesiastes has consistently said that man is "dust" (3:20). The words *Adam* and *dust* are semantically linked because man was made from the dust and is heading back to the dust due to the fact that in Eden he tried to contend with God, who is stronger than man! Who knows what is good for Adam (6:12)? This phrase calls us back to the time before the fall when everything was pronounced good. Now, however, fallen Adam's days pass like a shadow. Only God can tell what will happen after we pass off the scene.

Recalling the curse and how things were "good" prior to the fall causes us to long for the promised Savior implied in Genesis 3:15 who is to come and reverse the curse. That is exactly what Jesus came to do. This is illustrated so beautifully by the "3 Circles" gospel presentation

(Scroggins, "3 Circles"). The first circle shows that God has a design for everything in His world. God intends the material gifts He gives us to be used in certain ways that will cause us to flourish. Thus, he has a design for sex, food, relationships, work, and yes, money. These things are not "good" or "bad" in and of themselves. They can be used in good and godly ways that benefit us or in evil and sinful ways that harm us.

The second circle shows that our departure from God's design, which the Bible calls "sin," inevitably leads us into brokenness because we are not using things as God designed them to be used. For example, God gave us food as a gift to be used for nourishment, pleasure, and fellowship. But when we overindulge, which the Bible calls "gluttony," it causes brokenness in our lives, like body-image problems or health problems. Or if we misuse food in terms of anorexia or bulimia, brokenness looks like health problems or psychological problems. The same is true of money. When we do not use money as God designed—for provision, contentment, and generosity—then we become broken. Thus, love of money, hoarding, and failure to be content causes all of the harm we have seen in Ecclesiastes 5–6. It makes us miserable, lonely, insecure, and distrustful.

The problem is that we try all kinds of things to get out of the brokenness, but we just end up more broken. Some think they are empty and broken simply because they do not have enough things. They try to make more money and consume more goods, but it never fills the void. We cannot get out of the brokenness ourselves, and that is where the good news comes in. The final circle shows that Jesus died on the cross and rose from the dead, taking on Himself all of our sin and brokenness so that He could secure forgiveness, freedom, and a new start for us (2 Cor 5:17). We are called to recognize that we are broken, to repent of our sin and brokenness, and to trust in Jesus. When we do, He then makes us new creations who are filled with the Spirit and now have the ability to recover and pursue God's original design for our lives.

Conclusion

What this gospel transformation looks like with money is that now, instead of being miserly and stingy, we are content and generous. Paul points this out when in Ephesians 4 he talks about putting on the new man. What does that look like in regard to money? Ephesians 4:28 says, "The thief must no longer steal. Instead, he must do honest work with his own hands, so that he has something to share with anyone in need."

Made new in Christ, we are now free to recover God's design for our money, which means we are no longer stingy, but we work hard to provide for our families and to give generously to others. The gospel motivates all of this, as Paul says in 2 Corinthians 8:9: "For you know the grace of our Lord Jesus Christ: Though He was rich, for your sake He became poor, so that by His poverty you might become rich." The gospel transforms us into people who deeply enjoy what we have and generously meet the needs of others. When we see our hearts pulled away from that story, let us repent and find satisfaction in Christ!

Reflect and Discuss

1. When you read stories or watch movies about people who don't have a lot but are extremely happy, how do you feel?
2. Why do we think being wealthy applies only to the people in tax brackets higher than ours?
3. Solomon warns both the lazy man and the workaholic. How can we strike a balance in our lives?
4. What are some things in your life you thought would make you happy if you got them, but the happiness didn't last long?
5. In what ways do you have trouble "clocking out" when you leave work? What are some steps you should take to disengage from work and to rest better?
6. How can you fight against anxiety in the arena of money?
7. In what ways does contemplating death help you view money and possessions more biblically?
8. In what ways do meaningful relationships bring more joy than a lot of money and stuff?
9. Money can be a positive in the Bible. What are the ways we can view and use money rightly?
10. How does the gospel motivate us to be generous people?

Wisdom in a Meaningless World

ECCLESIASTES 7–11

Main Idea: Wisdom does not always work out immediately in this cursed world, but because of the gospel, wisdom does work out ultimately.

I.   **God Has a Design for Everything.**
II. **Sin Leads to Brokenness and Meaninglessness.**
III. **The Gospel Is the Answer to Our Brokenness and Meaninglessness.**
IV. **The Gospel Allows Us to Recover and Pursue God's Wise Design.**

I had an acquaintance in ministry—let's call him "Bob"—and he grew up much like me. He was born into a Christian home, he prayed to receive Christ as Savior at a young age, and he even felt called into ministry, so he pursued training in seminary. He got married to a Christian girl, had several kids with her, and pastored a couple of churches. However, through his time in seminary and then as a pastor of small churches, he became an aggressive atheist. The reasons he gives for his conversion to atheism are complex, but two of the reasons he gave for walking away from the faith are intriguing.

First, Bob became an atheist because he basically thinks Christianity "doesn't work." He gives evidence for this analysis starting with his childhood, years before he would abandon the faith. It started out with a really small thing before it progressed to bigger things. For example, when he was a boy, there was a girl he really liked, but she did not like him back. He prayed and prayed for God to help him win her over, but it never happened. Later on in life, when he began to pastor, he concluded that Christianity did not work because his churches did not grow. He observed that churches that rely on God for growth inevitably decline, while churches that rely on flashy methods and business models grow. Consider these statements.

> Looking back from my current perspective as an atheist, it
> is easy to spot a rather glaring problem within Christianity.
> Churches that relied on God for growth—sharing the gospel,
> being witnesses, trying to reach communities, but nonetheless

86

trusting that God would bring salvation—these churches were invariably declining churches. They relied on God, and were dying. On the other hand, growing churches were those which relied on flash teams or the latest business models or charismatic leadership. I am left with the clear conclusion that church growth has everything to do with the human component. Rely on magic methods and glittery gimmicks and people will come—just like they come to carnival rides and new restaurants. Rely on God to bring new fruit to a church and that church will soon wither away. People, not God, grow a church. . . .

I am still convinced of that last point. There is perhaps no greater evidence for atheism than the growth practices of today's large churches. Consider this dichotomy: churches that are growing do so through human efforts and human means, while churches trusting in God to bring revival and growth are in various stages of decline. Growing churches are very much centered on human effort and demonstrate clearly the power of charisma and community—the same characteristics one can find in any successful business endeavor without any need for the hand of God. Trust in God, and a church dies. Rely on the work of man, and a church just might make it. (Roberts, "My Journey")

Second, besides thinking that Christianity does not work, Bob's conversion to atheism was aided by the problem of evil and suffering in the world. He watched news reports of chemical attacks in the Middle East that killed hundreds of people at a time—most of whom went immediately to hell. He concluded there could not be a loving and just God in the world with hundreds of people being poisoned while they slept in their beds and then waking up in an eternal hell.

Sadly, while his wife is still a Christian trying to raise their children to know and love Jesus, Bob has become a convinced atheist, an evangelist for atheism, who attempts to convince others to walk away from a God whom he contends is not there anyway. Bob's story is not atypical. Many people struggle with the facts—the reality—that Christianity often does not seem to work and that there is much evil and suffering in the world. This reality drives some away from God, or at least it causes doubt. You get a cancer diagnosis, you get passed over for the promotion, you see that cheaters got an A in the class while you studied hard and got a B, or your kids have issues that unbelievers' kids do not, and these hardships can cause one to become skeptical and teeter on the edge of unbelief.

Solomon has the same problem in Ecclesiastes. He is teetering on the edge of unbelief because of the mess he sees in the world. He observes that living by God's wisdom does not always work out. The faithful often suffer and the wicked often prosper. This situation is futile! Therefore, Solomon takes on the role of a skeptic in order to observe the world and ask the question, Is there meaning in this cursed world? His experiment causes him to conclude that everything is meaningless. In Ecclesiastes 7–11 he observes the unjust nature of things, and he concludes again that everything is absurd. However, instead of this driving him away from God, it actually drives him to God in faith. Let's examine what he says so that during our struggles we can run to God instead of away from Him. Let's be instructed in wisdom in this meaningless world, a world that is not meaningless when God gets involved.

God Has a Design for Everything

God has a design for everything in creation, and the wisdom literature calls living according to that design "wisdom." God made the world to work a certain way, and you should live your life in that way—you should walk in wisdom (i.e., walk in the right way; Eccl 10:2)—because it will preserve your life. Ecclesiastes 7:12 states that "wisdom is protection . . . and the advantage of knowledge is that wisdom preserves the life of its owner." Living against God's design is foolishness because it threatens your life, whereas living according to it is wisdom because it leads to an abundant life.

There are many examples of proverbial wisdom in Ecclesiastes 7–11. These chapters often contrast wisdom and foolishness so that we can walk in wisdom. For example, Solomon says in Ecclesiastes 7:5, "It is better to listen to rebuke from a wise person than to listen to the song of fools." We should not be deceived by flattery, but instead we should appreciate hard truths (Dever, "The Ungodly"). Do not gain counsel from people who simply tell you what you want to hear; listen to those who will tell you the truth even when it is difficult, even when it hurts. Solomon gives much wisdom like this. He says not to be deceived by the love of money in ways that causes you to sin to get it (i.e., bribery or extortion; 7:7). Be patient instead of prideful (7:8). Be kind instead of angry (7:9). He says not to pine away for the good ol' days (7:10). People, especially Christians, often look back to some supposed golden age in our recent past where the world was as it should be. They observe the songs, the movies, and the sitcoms of yesterday in comparison with the ones today and conclude the world surely has gotten bad. For example, they will compare the Beatles' song about wanting to hold your hand with the overtly sexual lyrics in songs today and conclude things used to be much more wholesome. The problem is that the same era that gave us the Beatles also gave us songs like "Angel of the Morning," which is about a one-night stand. That era also gave us James Bond movies in which female characters had inappropriate names and sensual attire. Things have not been messed up only since the Sexual Revolution; things have been jacked up since Eden.

Solomon continues his wise discourse. He says it is wise to submit to authority, like the king's rule (8:2-7). We should submit to the governing authorities that God has placed in our lives—such as parents, pastors, and government officials—because God put them in place for our good (see 1 Pet 2:13–3:7). Solomon says a nation needs self-controlled rulers instead of rulers that are controlled by their appetites (Eccl 10:16-17). Solomon tells us to control our tongues and use our words wisely. He says not to speak too much (10:12-14). This theme is common in wisdom writings. There is sin in the multiplication of many words! Solomon tells us to avoid laziness (10:18) and to diversify business ventures to gain success (11:1-6) (Garrett, *Proverbs, Ecclesiastes, Song of Songs,* 338). Ecclesiastes 7–11 gives much wise counsel on the way we should live life!

This wise counsel helps you navigate your way through life in a way that protects you (7:12). For example, if you only gain counsel from the "yes men" chorus that you gather around you, then you will never be challenged when you are wrong, and that will lead to harmful decisions. Pastor Adrian Rogers said "A" leaders surround themselves with "A" companions. "B" leaders surround themselves with "C" companions! "A" companions will have the courage to speak truth into your life, even when it hurts to hear it.

If you sin to get money, then you may go to jail or pay a hefty fine. If you are angry instead of kind, then you will ruin your relationships. We must walk in wisdom according to God's design because that is how we will flourish in life.

However, while Solomon observes these wise principles, he also talks much about the limit of man's knowledge. Ecclesiastes 11:5 says, "Just as you don't know the path of the wind, or how bones develop in the womb of a pregnant woman, so you don't know the work of God who makes everything." Man's observations are limited to life lived "under the sun" in this cursed world, and even that is too much because we do not know the path the wind will take (11:5; cf. 8:17). Since our observation is limited, we cannot figure everything out. One of the main reasons we cannot figure everything out in this cursed world is because things do not always work out the way they are supposed to work out (8:14-17). Living by wisdom does not always make life go smoothly. Why? What is going on? Why is there suffering? Why do these wisdom principles not work? The problem is that humanity has departed from God's design. The Bible calls this departure "sin," and sin leads to brokenness and meaninglessness.

Sin Leads to Brokenness and Meaninglessness

Ecclesiastes has consistently written "meaningless" or "futile" over human existence. We could also describe this as brokenness—something is broken when it does not work right. When it comes to brokenness in this world, we need to realize two things. Sometimes we are broken because of our own sin, and sometimes we are broken because we live in a cursed, broken world.

Ecclesiastes makes something abundantly clear: all of humanity—including you—has sinned and departed from God's wise design for the world. When we rebel against our design, we end up broken. We know this to be true experientially. After all, anytime you attempt to use something in a way that its designer did not intend for it to be used, it gets broken or does not work. I remember as a teenager watching my younger brother try to cook a Pop-Tart for breakfast one morning. Apparently removing it from the wrapper and placing it in the toaster was too much of a chore, so instead he placed the Pop Tart, aluminum sleeve and all, in the microwave. When he hit start on the microwave, fireworks started going off in our house. Why? The makers of Pop Tarts did not design their wrappers to be heated in the microwave.

I have young daughters and a young son, so we often watch the Disney channel. I remember watching a show called *Doc McStuffins*, which is about a little girl who plays a doctor for toys, which means she fixes broken toys. In one episode a toy named "Rockin' Roxy," a pop star, got broken and could not sing any longer. She was so distraught she wanted to find something else to do with her life. Maybe she should be a police toy, a knight, or a gymnast. However, Doc explained to her that a "toy has to be what it was built to be," and then Doc fixed her. That may be a silly example, but it is true for humans as well. We must be who we were designed to be, and if we are not, then we will experience brokenness. Plus, we cannot fix our brokenness by trying to be something else. That will just make us more broken.

The problem is that we are all sinful and broken, and that hurts. So like Rockin' Roxy, we try to find ways out of our brokenness, but we just end up more and more broken. For example, some people think gender reassignment will fix their brokenness, but that only makes suicide 20 times more likely. Some people think intimacy will fix their brokenness so they go from relationship to relationship trying to fill the void, but they end up hurt and unsatisfied each time as they look harder and harder for something they will not find. Others look to success in a job, or making lots of money, or hundreds of other things, but these things never bring lasting satisfaction. So much of our futility and brokenness is due to our own sin and our own idolatry in which we turn good things into ultimate things. We worship money, pleasure, sex, success, power, and much more. Instead of seeing those things as gifts from God to be used as He intended, we see them as ultimate and seek to get from them what they cannot give. So often the things we think we want so badly fail to provide what we think they will, and we end up empty. That is the brokenness of departing from God's good design. We all sin, and we are all broken.

Ecclesiastes reveals we are broken because of our sin. Ecclesiastes 7:20 states, "There is certainly no righteous man on the earth who does good and never sins." That sounds like Romans 3:9-20. Ecclesiastes 7:29 says, "Only see this: I have discovered that God made people upright, but they pursued many schemes." The word translated "people" in the HCSB is literally the word *Adam* in Hebrew. God made Adam perfect in the beginning, but Adam pursued his own way rather than God's way. We have all joined our first parent in that rebellion, and thus we have all experienced brokenness!

Not only does Ecclesiastes 7:29 point out that we have all sinned; it also echoes back to the original sin in the fall, which leads to our second observation: Sometimes we are broken because we live in a world broken by the fall. Ecclesiastes talks much of man's sinfulness and how God has imposed a curse on the world (e.g., 1:13-15). God made the world crooked in response to Adam's sin (7:13), and man cannot fix it!

Solomon says, "Consider the work of God, for who can straighten out what He has made crooked?" All humans experience the meaninglessness and brokenness of this world where things do not work right. Sin and brokenness are equal-opportunity destroyers.

Yes, sometimes we are broken because of our own sin. For example, if you drive drunk and hurt someone, that is on you. If you cheat on your wife and lose your family, that is on you. But sometimes our brokenness is due to the sins done against us. For example, if you are abused, then that is someone sinning against you and breaking you. And yet, sometimes our brokenness is simply due to the sin of Adam and the fact that we live in a broken world.

Ecclesiastes points this out repeatedly in chapters 7–11. Things do not work the way we think they should. The righteous suffer while the wicked prosper (7:15). The wisdom literature honestly recognizes that things do not always work out as they ought immediately in this world. Some scholars want to act like Ecclesiastes is a corrective to the overly optimistic wisdom of Proverbs, but that is simply not the case. Proverbs recognizes these discrepancies and points them out as well, but Ecclesiastes simply dwells on them more. For example, Ecclesiastes 8:10-17 emphasizes this reality.

> In such circumstances, I saw the wicked buried. They came and went from the holy place, and they were praised in the city where they did so. This too is futile. Because the sentence against a criminal act is not carried out quickly, the heart of people is filled with the desire to commit crime. Although a sinner commits crime a hundred times and prolongs his life, yet I also know that it will go well with God-fearing people, for they are reverent before Him. However, it will not go well with the wicked, and they will not lengthen their days like a shadow, for they are not reverent before God.
>
> There is a futility that is done on the earth: there are righteous people who get what the actions of the wicked deserve, and there are wicked people who get what the actions of the righteous deserve. I say that this too is futile. So I commended enjoyment because there is nothing better for man under the sun than to eat, drink, and enjoy himself, for this will accompany him in his labor during the days of his life that God gives him under the sun.
>
> When I applied my mind to know wisdom and to observe the activity that is done on the earth (even though one's eyes do not close in sleep day or night), I observed all the work of God and concluded

that man is unable to discover the work that is done under the sun.
Even though a man labors hard to explore it, he cannot find it; even if
the wise man claims to know it, he is unable to discover it.

Solomon observes hypocrites who are praised in the world. These are wicked people who play the religious game—coming and going from the holy place—acting like they are godly when they are not. Yet they are praised in life and honored in death with a proper burial, and because of this, others join them in their wickedness. This reality could describe a lot of nominal Christianity in America and even throughout the world.

Also, Solomon observes that because retribution is not carried out immediately, people increase evil (8:11). Why not join the evil people when they are the ones who prosper? They have a good reputation, get lots of affirmation, and are even seen as religious. Justice deferred is an encouragement to practice evil (Dever, "The Ungodly"). We see this truth with our children. When Judson walks over to take Maddy or Emma's iPad, if I laugh at him instead of disciplining him, what will happen? He will do it again! Deferred punishments encourage wrongdoing—that is the way of this cursed world on the small scale in our homes and even on a bigger scale in our culture and society. Court systems that do not swiftly and justly sentence criminals remove the deterrent to crime. That is even true when it comes to the ultimate Judge, God. When God in His patience passes over sin to a delayed judgment, yes, His mercy causes some to repent, but it also causes some to become entrenched in their wickedness because there is no immediate accountability. They need to be reminded of the truth of 2 Peter 3:9-10.

The Lord does not delay His promise, as some understand delay,
but is patient with you, not wanting any to perish but all to come to
repentance.
But the Day of the Lord will come like a thief; on that day the
heavens will pass away with a loud noise, the elements will burn and
be dissolved, and the earth and the works on it will be disclosed.

Shockingly, not only is there no justice, but sinners prolong their lives while the righteous receive the retribution the wicked deserve (8:12,14). We see this reality and we say, "That's not fair!" But that is the world we live in.

The problem is not just the random injustice of things not working out right but also the ultimate mystery that happens to all of us. Death is the ultimate problem, and it comes to all regardless of how we live.

You may not experience brokenness until death, but it will come to all of us regardless of how successful we are in this life. Your effort makes no difference. Solomon says in Ecclesiastes 9:11-12 that no matter how well you live this life, you will eventually be caught by time and chance. The Grim Reaper is faster than us all. He never grows weary, and when he shows up, we often never saw him coming!

> *Again I saw under the sun that the race is not to the swift, or the battle to the strong, or bread to the wise, or riches to the discerning, or favor to the skillful; rather, time and chance happen to all of them. For man certainly does not know his time: like fish caught in a cruel net or like birds caught in a trap, so people are trapped in an evil time as it suddenly falls on them.*

Therefore, Solomon contemplates a world with suffering, injustice, and death to expose us to the absurdity of life. Tim Keller says that life is a "crapshoot" ("Search for Justice"). He explains that you might see on the news that a terrorist walks onto a bus in the Middle East and blows up dozens of people, so you say, "OK. I'm not gonna ride on buses in the Middle East." But people die in car crashes here every day. No man has power over the day of his death (8:8). Whether you are a terrorist, a victim, or a child who dies in a car crash, it makes no difference to Death. Thus, life just seems so tragic and meaningless. That is life in this cursed world. It does not work right, and this reality drives many people away from the faith. So what do we make of this brokenness and futility? Is there any hope?

The Gospel Is the Answer to Our Brokenness and Meaninglessness

Ecclesiastes 12 says Solomon's intention in this book is to shepherd us with these words (12:11). Thus, Solomon exposes us to the brokenness of the world—a brokenness that really hurts and brings emptiness—for the positive outcome of causing us not to build our lives on things or people other than God. Ecclesiastes is God's goodness to us because He refuses to allow us to wallow in our broken futility. In His love He frustrates us (Dever, "The Ungodly"). Our frustration over the absurdity of life drives us to God and His gospel. That is the answer to brokenness and meaninglessness.

Ecclesiastes encourages faith in God and His gospel in two ways here in Ecclesiastes 7–11. First, it reveals that God is in control and working

Ro. 8:28

things out according to His timing and plan. Therefore, Ecclesiastes 7:14-18 exhorts us to fear God.

> *In the day of prosperity be joyful, but in the day of adversity, consider: God has made the one as well as the other, so that man cannot discover anything that will come after him.*
>
> *In my futile life I have seen everything: there is a righteous man who perishes in spite of his righteousness, and there is a wicked man who lives long in spite of his evil. Don't be excessively righteous, and don't be overly wise. Why should you destroy yourself? Don't be excessively wicked, and don't be foolish. Why should you die before your time? It is good that you grasp the one and do not let the other slip from your hand. For the one who fears God will end up with both of them.*

There is much we could dig into in this passage, but let's focus on the big points. As we saw in Ecclesiastes 3, God's plan for our lives includes both our prosperity and our adversity. He mixes both together to bring about something beautiful, even though we cannot see what that is right now from our small vantage point (cf. 3:11-15). Our wisdom is limited (cf. 8:14-17), so we need to trust God. That is the point of the book. After all, the fear of the Lord is the beginning of wisdom (Prov 1:7). As Ecclesiastes 7:14-18 points out, the one who fears God will avoid both self-righteousness and foolishness. That is the way we are to live life—trusting in Almighty God.

Tim Keller explains that this approach is helpful for people who deal with the problem of evil and injustice at an intellectual level. If, theoretically, evil and suffering are a problem for you, then there has to be a big God out there with a plan for everything that happens ("Search for Justice"). If there is a God, then evil is a problem. But if there is no God, then evil is not a problem because if there is no God, then there is no such thing as evil. The idea of justice is a cruel mirage. Solomon gets at this reality in Ecclesiastes 9:4 when he says it is better to be a scoundrel like a dog and save your skin than noble like a lion and dead. If this life is all there is and if there is no God, then there is no right and wrong. There is no reason to work for justice or fair treatment of others. Better to be a utilitarian and save your own hide than risk it to save others and be dead.

Bob the atheist is concerned with the survival of the human species and with humans being good to one another. He writes of the importance of his atheism:

I came to realize that the stakes are terribly high, as high as the very survival of our species. Pascal's wager says that if there is no God, the worst possible consequence is that I won't go to heaven when I die. The real world says that if there is no God, but we act as if there is, then we as a species might well drive ourselves to extinction. This is not a remote hypothetical, this is a definite, looming threat. (Roberts, "Journey")

My question for him is, Why do you care? What does it matter? Why is it good that we survive as a species? Why should we be nice to one another? Should we not let the strong survive and the weak die off? If evil and suffering are a problem for you, then you must believe in God. There at least has to be a God out there big enough for you to get mad at. However, that answer to the problem of evil and suffering is a kind of intellectual answer that does little for people who actually suffer.

The good news is that Solomon does address injustice at the personal level. He tells a story in Ecclesiastes 9:13-16.

> I have observed that this also is wisdom under the sun, and it is significant to me: There was a small city with few men in it. A great king came against it, surrounded it, and built large siege works against it. Now a poor wise man was found in the city, and he delivered the city by his wisdom. Yet no one remembered that poor man. And I said, "Wisdom is better than strength, but the wisdom of the poor man is despised, and his words are not heeded."

These verses tell the story of a poor, wise man who saves the city but is rejected. The passage is deeply puzzling because the people were indifferent to the hero who saved them. Sinclair Ferguson calls this passage a prophecy. He writes, "Whose name most naturally comes to mind when we hear of a poor man, full of wisdom, who became a savior but whose life and teaching have been rejected?" (*Pundit's Folly*, 51). The answer is obviously "Jesus!" Jesus is the Wisdom of God (1 Cor 1:24,30) and the Savior we scorn.

Not only is Jesus the designer behind creation, but He is also the one who enters creation and lives out that design. He took on flesh (John 1:14), and He grew in wisdom and stature (Luke 2:52). He is greater than Solomon because he never faltered from His wisdom (Matt 12:42). He is the answer to the limited knowledge of mankind. Since we could not go up to God to get wisdom, God sent His Son to us with His wisdom (Prov 30:1-4). Wisdom is ultimately not a thing, not an idea, and not a concept; wisdom is a Person. We are sinful fools who will never be wise apart from Jesus Christ.

The gospel teaches that Jesus took on our sin, our folly, and our death to save us from them. In a world filled with suffering and injustice, He suffered the greatest injustice the world has ever seen—the murder of God the Creator! God did not remain distant from the problem of evil and suffering. He became part of it so that He could one day do away with it. We can hold on to our faith in times of pain because we serve a God—a Savior—who has experienced rejection and pain. This is so beautifully seen in Edward Shillito's poem "Jesus of the Scars."

> If we have never sought, we seek Thee now;
> Thine eyes burn through the dark, our only stars;
> We must have sight of thorn-pricks on Thy brow,
> We must have Thee, O Jesus of the Scars.
>
> The heavens frighten us; they are too calm;
> In all the universe we have no place.
> Our wounds are hurting us; where is the balm?
> Lord Jesus, by Thy Scars, we claim Thy grace.
>
> If, when the doors are shut, Thou drawest near,
> Only reveal those hands, that side of Thine;
> We know to-day what wounds are, have no fear,
> Show us Thy Scars, we know the countersign.
>
> The other gods were strong; but Thou wast weak;
> They rode, but Thou didst stumble to a throne;
> But to our wounds only God's wounds can speak,
> And not a god has wounds, but Thou alone.

Jesus is the Savior who rescues us from brokenness. Jesus is the wise man who makes us wise. Jesus is the poor man who makes us rich. And yet He was rejected too! Mark Dever points out that Isaiah 53 explains the wisdom and foolishness of Ecclesiastes 7–11. The righteous man got what the wicked deserved, so the wicked could get what the righteous deserve (Dever, "The Ungodly"). The poor, wise Savior who rescued the world is rejected and despised because the wisdom of God is foolishness to the world and the wisdom of the world is foolishness to God (1 Cor 1:18-25). It pleased God to save through a cross that looked like foolishness. Turn to Jesus, and He can free you from your brokenness and meaninglessness. Let Him turn your foolishness into wisdom.

The Gospel Allows Us to Recover and Pursue God's Wise Design

In Christ we get to recover and pursue God's design for our lives. That means living out the wisdom of Ecclesiastes, which looks like contentment with what you have, kindness toward others instead of anger, the ability to control your tongue, a good work ethic, patience rather than arrogantly demanding what you want, and rightly submitting to authority. When you follow God's design in this fallen world, things may not always work out *immediately*, but they will work out *ultimately*. God will make all things new in the end, and He will set all things right to His original design. Ecclesiastes 8:12-13 and 12:13-14, among other texts, say there will be a final reckoning where all is set right and made new. The wicked will not prosper forever, and the righteous who are in Christ will not suffer forever.

We can trust these things are true not simply because we fear a sovereign God who is in control, but we can trust these things because we also trust in a God who suffered in order to end the suffering and chaos of this cursed world one day, a God who was treated unjustly to end injustice one day, a God with scars! So repent and believe the gospel. Allow God to empower you to live out His wise design for the world by the power of His Spirit!

Reflect and Discuss

1. What are some things that can cause you or those you know to doubt the truth claims of Christianity?

2. What have you observed that causes you to think the world does not work right?

3. Growing up, what did you think of the "rules" in the Bible? Did you see them as freeing or constricting? How does viewing them as God's design for your flourishing alter your view?

4. What are some examples of wise counsel in Ecclesiastes 7–11? How can we live them out practically?

5. What are some things you would love to know the answer to, but you know you will not get the answer? What does this lack of knowledge tell you about the human condition?

6. What are some practical ways going against God's design hurts us?

7. What are some ways we try to get out of brokenness but make things worse?

8. Many people think they suffer because of some unknown sin they committed that God is mad about and wants to punish. How does the teaching in Ecclesiastes 7–11 alter that view?

9. In what ways does the meaninglessness of life show us the goodness of God?

10. How does knowing you serve a God who has suffered in your place and on your behalf aid you in dealing with suffering in your life?

Death Is Meaningless without Jesus

ECCLESIASTES 9:1-10

Main Idea: Death can render all of life's actions meaningless, but Jesus gives an abundant and eternal life.

I. **Death Can Render All of Life's Actions Meaningless (9:1-6).**
II. **Death Can Render All of Life's Actions Meaningful (9:7-10).**
III. **Jesus Delivers from Death and Gives Abundant, Eternal Life.**

The first time I ever really encountered death was when one of my mom's best friends, Kathy Stanley, died from cancer. I was about nine or ten years old when she died. It was such a shock because our families were so close. Every Sunday night after the evening church service, we would all go back to our house, order Little Caesar's pizza, and hang out. The Stanleys had two boys about our age, and we loved spending time together. When Kathy was initially diagnosed with cancer, the treatments worked and she recovered, but eventually the cancer came back. And it came back with a vengeance. One night my dad called a family meeting, and we all gathered in the living room for him to tell us that Kathy had died, leaving behind her husband and two young boys. Not only was that the first time in my life I really had to deal with death, but when my dad did the eulogy during the funeral, it was the first time I ever saw my dad cry. It was unsettling.

One thing is abundantly clear: death is a predator that tracks us down. We can't outrun death no matter how much kale we eat, how many medicines we take, how many diets we try, how many botox injections we receive, or how many workout programs we do. Death really seems to render life senseless because it cancels out everything we do, and all our human effort is not the ultimate factor in whether we die or live. Effort, in the end, has nothing to do with it. There are really fit people whose hearts give out and they die young, and there are chain smokers who live into their nineties.

That is Solomon's point here in Ecclesiastes. It does not matter how wise you are, how much money you make, how much comfort you have, how successful you are, how religious you are, or how cleanly you live your life. Death is the great equalizer. This human assassin comes looking for us all, and he will find you. Death robs your life of value. So what do we do about this? Ecclesiastes 9:1-10 gives an intriguing analysis and outlook on life and death.

Death Can Render All of Life's Actions Meaningless
ECCLESIASTES 9:1-6

This passage is basically the crescendo for Solomon's point about the meaninglessness of life. If this cursed world is all there is, and there is no God or life beyond the grave, then everything is meaningless. Death cancels all of our actions. Solomon drives us to the reality of death in this passage so he can tell us how to handle death.

Solomon was a sage who methodically examined the reality of death in this cursed world. He analyzed how the righteous and the wise and their actions are in God's hands and how man does not know if that indicates God's love or hate (9:1). Here is the basic idea: God sovereignly rules over our lives, which according to Ecclesiastes 3 are subject to His timing, and our surroundings give us no clue as to what God really thinks of us (Enns, *Ecclesiastes*, 82). We cannot use our circumstances to determine if God loves us or hates us, accepts us or rejects us.

This concept runs against the grain of a lot of Christian silliness that says, "If you are faithful, then you will be prosperous." Many preachers and churches claim that if you really love God, then you will be happy, healthy, and wealthy. Books tell you that if you pray certain prayers then your territory will be expanded. But as Matt Chandler points out, John the Baptist was godly and did not get his territory expanded; he got his head cut off ("Daily Contact"). Being in God's hand is not synonymous with prosperity, health, or a pain-free life (Hunt, *Ecclesiastes*, 51). God's people do suffer, but we trust that Jesus is enough, that He is in control, and that His timing and plan are best in the midst of the suffering!

Therefore, since godliness is not a guarantee of prosperity or comfort, we cannot look at our circumstances to determine if God is for or against us. The main place we see this kind of chaos is death because it comes to all regardless of how they live (9:2). To demonstrate the truth that everyone is affected by death, Solomon gives six meristic pairs to show the totality of death's reign. It does not matter if you are righteous or wicked, good or evil, clean or unclean, one who sacrifices or one who does not, a good person or a sinner, or one who makes oaths or one who does not. Death comes to all. This statement is significant coming from an Israelite because Solomon is basically saying that being an obedient Israelite really amounts to nothing at the end of the day (Enns, *Ecclesiastes*, 94–95).

This situation proves that life's circumstances give no clue as to what God really thinks of us. After all, the things that are supposed to matter most to Him—sacrifices, oaths, and living by the law—seem to make no real difference (Kidner, *Ecclesiastes*, 82). Regardless of how moral or religious we are, we all die. Again, death is the great equalizer. Ecclesiastes has written meaninglessness or futility over everything, and death is the climax of life's absurdity. The cynical bumper sticker says it well: "Life is a dog [actually a more colorful word] and then you die." Why bother to live a godly life when we all end up the same way in the end (Hunt, *Ecclesiastes*, 52)? Death's tyranny shows there is a curse on the world and something has gone terribly wrong.

Kidner argues that Ecclesiastes 9:3 calls the universality of death the greatest evil in the world (Kidner, *Ecclesiastes*, 82). We were made to live (Gen 1–2), but we all end up dying (Gen 3). Solomon adds the reason we all die: Adam's sons are full of evil and go to the dead. Solomon makes an explicit connection with the fall. We have inherited corruption, sin, and death from our first father, Adam (cf. Rom 5:12-19). If any of us doubt this reality, we can just look at our children and see that we all inherit a sin nature. The other day my 18-months-old son, Judson, wanted to go up the stairs by himself, which is a bad idea because unattended he might break something—most likely himself. So I told him, no and started to carry him back down the stairs. When I picked him up, he screamed and pulled my hair. Where did he learn that? He's never seen his parents do that. Never one time have I pulled my wife's hair because I wasn't getting my way. He did not have to be taught to do that because he is a born sinner. Not only are we all sinners, but also, as was said in the beginning, the wages of sin is death (Rom 6:23; cf. Gen 2:17; Rom 5:12). Ecclesiastes 9 makes clear that all have sinned and fallen short of God's glory, and the wages for that sin is death for all. Because I sin, death will come for me. Because you sin, death will come for you.

In Ecclesiastes 9:4-6 the author states the relative advantage of life over death. Life is slightly more advantageous than death despite the meaninglessness of life in this cursed world. The reason for the minor advantage is that those who are still alive have hope because a live dog is better than a dead lion. First of all, I love this verse because it is biblical proof for something we all know to be true—dogs are better than cats, even big cats! Second, modern persons like ourselves do not really understand what is going on in this verse because we think of dogs as "man's best friend." Dogs are cute, domesticated animals that often live in our homes and lie on our furniture, but in the ancient world dogs were scavengers—like vultures or rats in our society. Dogs would feast on dead flesh, as when the dogs licked up Ahab's blood or ate Queen Jezebel's corpse (1 Kgs 22; 2 Kgs 9). Lions, by contrast, are powerful and stately. The author's point is that even a disgusting scoundrel of a person is better off than a noble person who is dead (Keller, "Search for Justice"). Why? It is better to be morally dirty and alive than noble and dead because the dead have no consciousness, they have no reward, they are forgotten. All of their emotions, both positive and negative, are gone, and they no longer have any portion of anything allocated to them under the sun (Eccl 9:5-6). Again, if life under the sun is all there is, then death wipes away everything—all our memories, all our possessions, all our feelings, and all our relationships. Plus, if life under the sun is all there is, there is nothing beyond the grave. On the other hand, the living at least have hope because they can be conscious of the fact that they will die. That is the advantage. The living have a chance to reckon with the reality of death and do something about it (Garrett, *Proverbs, Ecclesiastes, Song of Songs*, 331). They can enjoy life as a gift, repent of evil, and live differently in the face of death.

The problem is that most people, instead of reckoning with death, waste the little time they have on planet Earth with distractions (Garrett, *Proverbs, Ecclesiastes, Song of Songs*, 331). Many do not think about death but instead live as if they have an endless supply of days ahead of them. Solomon calls this foolishness. Not contemplating death causes you to be an unwise person. On the other hand, some look at death and say silly things like, "Live every day as if it were your last!" So many movies are made with this premise, and so many "poppy" sermons have the same kind of application. So much of Christian "teaching" has become one-liner pop-culture fortune cookies. No! Do not live every day as if it were your last. If tomorrow were truly your last day, then there would be no reason to go to work, pay your bills, do your chores, study for an exam, or a thousand other things we must do. Do not live every day as if it were your last, but do live as if you have a set number of days. Live as if you do not get an endless supply. Living your life with this in mind is wise because it will help you not be careless with your spouse, miss out on time with your children, be indifferent at your job, or other such distractions.

Solomon turns now to instruct us on how to live life in the face of death's certainty. While death can render all of life's actions meaningless . . .

Death Can Render All of Life's Actions Meaningful
ECCLESIASTES 9:7-10

Wow! These ideas may sound contradictory, but the reality of death can render life meaningless or incredibly meaningful. That is Solomon's argument here, an argument he has made throughout the book. Ecclesiastes 7:2 says, "It is better to go to a house of mourning than to go to a house of feasting, since that is the end of all mankind, and the living should take it to heart." Contemplate death and take it to heart so you can enjoy life. That is his point. Go to a funeral rather than a party so that you can contemplate your frailty and finitude as a means to live wisely and enjoy life.

Facing death has a way of making you enjoy life more. One Sunday morning, a few years back, I received a call at 4:45 a.m. from my associate pastor who told me that a woman in our church named Katy, who was about 20 weeks pregnant at the time, had suffered a massive brain aneurism and was on life support at the hospital. I was devastated to receive that call. Katy and her husband TJ had two children and a third on the way. I had led Katy to the Lord and baptized her. It was shocking and heartbreaking to hear what had happened. As soon as the morning services were over, I rushed down to the hospital. I remember walking into the ICU waiting room, and the first person I saw was Katy's mother-in-law. When she saw me, she screamed at me, "No! There is no God if this is happening!" I just hugged her and tried to console her. The situation was grim. Katy's brain function had ceased. They were keeping her plugged into a machine in order to try to get the baby to a viable delivery date. Unfortunately, due to the trauma, the baby could not stay in. She was delivered and within an hour died. I was in the room looking at this father holding his dead baby girl in his arms, his wife in the room next door about to die, and I just sobbed. He let me hold his baby girl, and it broke my heart. A little later on I prayed over the family before they unplugged Katy, and she died within seconds.

A few days later I would perform a funeral for a young mom with her dead baby girl lying on her chest in an open casket. It was probably the hardest thing I have ever had to do in ministry. However, when I got home from the hospital that first night, I squeezed my wife, I squeezed my girls, I fell to the ground with them while tears streamed down my cheeks, and I would not let go! The gut-wrenching reality of death caused me to love, enjoy, and appreciate my family in a way I had not just 24 hours earlier.

Solomon tells us that in the face of death's harsh reality, we should enjoy life. He commands us to seize the day—carpe diem. As Murphy points out, the content of these verses is the same as previous sections, but the tone is different because it is in imperative language (Murphy, *Proverbs, Ecclesiastes, Song of Songs*, 209). Solomon gives a representative list of six things we should enjoy in life.

First, he says to eat your bread with pleasure (v. 7). Enjoy your meals, eat good food, and see meals as a chance for fellowship. Food is a wonderful gift from God meant to bring us nourishment but also pleasure, taste, variety, and an opportunity for relationships. God gives us the gift of food for us to enjoy it as a means to worship Him with grateful hearts for His provision and creativity.

Second, he says to drink your wine with a glad heart for God has already approved of what you do (v. 7). The consumption of beverage alcohol is a controversial issue in our day for many reasons. One reason I have seen up close and personal is the damaging effects of alcohol on families. My mom spent a decade of her life in the Georgia Baptist Children's Home because of alcoholic parents who could not care for her. Because of many people's experiences, the issue of beverage alcohol is touchy and painful. Yet we do need to adopt a biblical approach to this subject as we let the lens of God's authority determine how we view our own experiences. We need to be honest and open about what the Bible says.

On the one hand, the Bible strongly condemns drunkenness in any form. On the other hand it is open to moderate, self-controlled drinking. I think when it comes to the diverse approaches to alcohol among Christians that Paul's instruction to the church at Rome in Romans 14 is helpful for us. Paul instructs believers in the Roman church not to judge one another by what one eats or drinks (Rom 14:1-19), and he also says not to do something that would cause a weaker brother to stumble (Rom 14:21). Thus, one could choose a teetotaler position for wisdom's and witness's sake, or one could choose a moderation position. Both positions could be perfectly biblical. The larger issue for Paul is that it should not become a reason for division in the church. Cut each other some slack! Be mindful of your brothers' weak points. But above all, be loving toward one another recognizing there will be different ways the conscience is affected by this issue.

For Solomon's part here in Ecclesiastes, wine was simply the drink of choice in ancient Israel, and so he says that part of enjoying life is enjoying a tasty beverage. That could apply to all kinds of drink options we have today. Diet Coke is certainly on my dad's tasty beverage list!

Third, he tells them to wear white all the time (v. 8), which means to wear festive clothing. The instruction to wear white is culturally conditioned. White was the garment of choice because of the hot temperatures in the Middle East (Murphy, *Proverbs, Ecclesiastes, Song of Songs,* 209). The idea is to wear celebratory clothes that fit your cultural context.

Fourth, he says to put oil on your head (v. 8). Again, the Middle East is arid, and skin can get dry. Oil was a means of protecting the skin in the Middle Eastern heat (Longman, *Ecclesiastes,* 230). Protect your skin from the heat so you can enjoy life. These last two commands would be good ideas for guys trying to get dates. Dress nice; put something smooth and nice smelling on your skin.

Fifth, he says to enjoy your wife (v. 9). Love your wife, be her best friend, and enjoy her physically, emotionally, and spiritually. This is not only practical advice for a good marriage and a happy life, but it is also a command from God. Read what Paul writes to the Corinthian church in 1 Corinthians 7:3-5, and then remind yourself of James's admonition that we not merely be hearers of the Word but doers also (Jas 1:22). Paul writes,

> *A husband should fulfill his marital responsibility to his wife, and likewise a wife to her husband. A wife does not have the right over her own body, but her husband does. In the same way, a husband does not have the right over his own body, but his wife does. Do not deprive one another sexually—except when you agree for a time, to devote yourselves to prayer. Then come together again; otherwise, Satan may tempt you because of your lack of self-control.*

As husbands read those verses, they are thinking to themselves, *We are going to start doing family devotionals tonight, and we are going to read 1 Corinthians 7, and I'm gonna say "Honey, Paul said we need to have a lot of sex, and we want to be a biblical family, so let's not just be hearers of the Word."*

Solomon says enjoy your wife, and he means it! (But guys, never lose sight of Eph 5:25-33!)

Sixth, enjoy your work and activities (v. 10). Find a job, find a hobby, and find activities to do with your family. Do life with all you have because death is near. Solomon paints the picture of fully enjoying life. Eat good meals, have a pure life, enjoy a loving marriage, and find a good job (Hunt, *Ecclesiastes*, 56). As Mark Driscoll points out, get dressed up nice, put on something that makes you smell good, and take your wife to a nice meal (Driscoll, "Cleaning Your Plate").

We skipped over a key phrase in Ecclesiastes 9:7 without comment. Solomon tells the reader to enjoy life—eat and drink well—because "God has already accepted your works." Wow! God favors our enjoying the gifts He has given to us. So let's be clear: it is not a sin to enjoy life (Garrett, *Proverbs, Ecclesiastes, Song of Songs*, 331). Many in America were raised on a brand of Christianity that communicated life is a drag and holiness is boring. Many were taught that holiness in Christianity means having no fun—holiness is found only in abstaining from fun (Driscoll, "Cleaning Your Plate"). Some were taught that if it feels good, makes you happy, or you enjoy it, then it is a sin, so get rid of it, and stop doing it. Solomon tells us the exact opposite. God wants you to enjoy life, He wants it to feel good, and He wants you to be happy in Him. God is the author of fun, and He gave these gifts to be enjoyed as He intended. After all, He created paradise where there was a garden with tons of acreage, with all the food you could ever eat, and then He put a husband and wife in that paradise with no clothes on (Gen 1–2)! That sounds like a pretty good deal to me; that sounds like a wonderful retirement plan! Solomon encourages us to enjoy life while we can because death is an enemy that will steal everything from us at any moment.

Ecclesiastes exposes us to the meaningless and fleeting nature of life in this cursed world for the purpose of causing us to long for something beyond the grave, and we find that here in this last point.

Jesus Delivers from Death and Gives Abundant, Eternal Life

Ecclesiastes depicts in great detail the curse of sin and death. Death's tyranny makes life meaningless because if this life is all there is, then death cancels everything out. You cannot take your money with you. Your legacy will ultimately be forgotten. Nothing you did really seems to matter. Some scholars look at this and say Ecclesiastes believes there is nothing beyond the grave, but that is wrong. Ecclesiastes does not teach annihilation; it teaches uncertainty. Solomon purposefully takes on this particular human perspective, and he says we cannot know for sure if anything lies beyond death because none of us has ever gone there and come back.

However, we do know something is out there, and we long for it because eternity is in our hearts (3:11). What Ecclesiastes aches for, the New Testament presents to us. Paul wrote to the church at Rome to tell them that death did enter the world through one man, but life also came into the world through one man (Rom 5:12-21). We sin and die because of what we inherited from Adam, and so we need to be redeemed. Yes, the wages of sin is death, but the gift of God is eternal life through Jesus Christ our Lord (Rom 6:23). The question that needs to be raised is, How does Jesus redeem us from the curse of death? He did so by taking the curse of sin and death on Himself at Golgotha (Gal 3:13). As Mark Driscoll said, "The only way to get rid of death is to get rid of sin" ("Cleaning Your Plate"). Jesus took care of both sin and death at the cross and through His resurrection. There is one man who did not decay into the dust (Ps 16:10). There is one man who did not suffer the seemingly irreversible fate of death. He is the promised Deliverer of Genesis 3:15 who rolls back the curse of sin and death. The promise of the New Testament is that those who are in Him will be raised from the dead.

However, the promise is not just for eternal life; the promise is also for abundant life (John 10:10)—living life to the fullest as it was meant to be lived. From the beginning God meant for us to live life to the fullest: eating, drinking, loving, and working (Greidanus, *Preaching Christ*, 225–26). However, the fall stole all of that and so much more. Now, instead of using God's gifts rightly as a means to express gratitude and worship to Him, we use the gifts in rebellious and harmful ways. Food becomes gluttony, wine becomes drunkenness, sex becomes adultery, and work becomes an excuse for laziness or being a workaholic. We have rebelled against God's good design, and as a result we are broken.

The good news is that Jesus came to redeem us so that we can begin to live according to God's good design. He did not just die and rise again to forgive our sins; He also died and rose to conform His followers to His image (Rom 8:29), which means a new empowerment by the Spirit to live according to God's design. This design of enjoying life as God's image bearers is seen so clearly in the life of Jesus. He came feeding the five thousand and turning water into wine. He came eating and drinking—after all, He was accused of being a glutton and a drunk, even though He was not one (Matt 11:19). He came pursuing a bride (Eph 5:22-33), and He did the work His Father gave Him to do (John 9:4). He overthrew the curse so we can live redeemed lives in conformity to His image. Now, in Christ, we can live life to the full—eating, drinking, loving, and working in redeemed ways. We see glimpses of this edenic paradise that we came from and are heading to in churches that eat bread with glad hearts (Acts 2:46), in marriages that reflect the gospel, and in workers who provide for their children.

Conclusion

In the Old Testament Wisdom literature especially, there is a longing for eternal life. But it is not to "fly away" into some body-less existence. What they hoped for was a continued existence within creation (i.e., under the sun). They wanted a return to Eden—to live forever in a good creation. The New Testament says that is exactly what will happen. Those who are in Christ will live forever in a new creation (Rev 21–22), bodily raised from the dead. The world is heading to a paradise where we will eat, drink, love, and work to the glory of God and our own joy. We get to practice for the kingdom right now by enjoying life to the full in light of Christ's resurrection and triumph over death. As Russ Moore tweets, "Let us eat, drink and be merry for yesterday we were dead, but today we are alive!" (Twitter).

Reflect and Discuss

1. When did you have to face the reality of death for the first time? How did that experience make you feel?
2. What are some ways people try to flee from and escape death?
3. Have you ever used your circumstances to gauge how God feels about you at a given time? Why do you think we are so prone to do that?
4. Does Solomon teach here in Ecclesiastes 9 what so many song lyrics say, "Only the good die young"? How does Solomon's teaching in Ecclesiastes 9 teach us about the timing of people's death?
5. According to Ecclesiastes 9, as well as the rest of the Bible, why do we all die?
6. According to Solomon in Ecclesiastes 9, why is being alive, even as a scoundrel, better than being dead?

7. How can contemplating death cause you to enjoy life more?
8. Were you raised in a faith tradition that taught or implied that walking with God means not doing anything that feels good? Why do you think the church has often defaulted to that position?
9. How does Jesus rescue us from the curse of death?
10. How can you fully enjoy life in a godly way? What does the "abundant life" look like according to Ecclesiastes 9?

Aging Is Meaningless without Jesus

ECCLESIASTES 11:7–12:14

Main Idea: You can enjoy life in the face of aging and death if you turn to God through Jesus Christ.

I.   **Enjoy Life as God Intended (11:7-10).**
II. **Turn to God Now before Aging Robs You (12:1-7).**
III. **Trust in Jesus as Your Savior and Sage (12:8-14).**

A recent article showed that leading men in movies age, but their love interests do not (Buchanan, "Leading Men Age"). For example, while Denzel Washington is pushing 60, the starlet who acts opposite of him is usually 35 and under. Or consider Harrison Ford, who stars opposite love interests that are usually at least 15 years younger than him, if not more, or Liam Neeson's last movie in which he was 25 years older than his love interest, and on and on we might go.

Our culture is unique from many cultures in the world in that we do not prize age. Whereas many other cultures see age as a sign of wisdom and the elderly as those who should be honored, we do everything we can to marginalize the aged. We do everything we can to ignore aging. We ignore it by only putting "beautiful" and "young looking" people in movies, in advertisements, and in our magazines. We do it with billions of dollars spent every year on botox injections and plastic surgery. As Dolly Parton once said, "It cost a fortune to look this cheap." We do it with computer enhancements on photo spreads, photo shopping out unsightly images. We attempt to ignore aging with medicines, diets, workouts, and creams. If we are young, we ignore that aging is a reality at all. The young usually think they have an endless supply of days ahead of them.

Why do we do this? Why do we ignore aging? The reason we ignore aging is that we fear death, and since aging reminds us of our mortality, we desperately try to escape it. Yet no matter how much effort we exert to be healthy and safe, the bottom line is that we get about 100 years max in this world. That is why Five for Fighting says in the song "100 Years" that there is nothing better than being 15. The song talks about how brief life is, and so your teen years and your early twenties feel so great because you have time to live life, to make dumb choices and recover from them. Life moves so fast from getting married to having kids and starting a family to hitting your midlife crisis. Then, before you know it, you are a senior adult, and the sun is setting on your life. If this world is all there is and you only get about 100 years, then being 15 is the best thing in the world because you have all of your time, possibilities, decisions, and life goals out in front of you for the taking. We prize youth because we fear the fleeting nature of life and the finality of death.

Solomon has made the foreboding point throughout Ecclesiastes that life is fleeting and vain because our soon-coming death renders all our actions meaningless. Our short life gives way to the eternal home of death. It is a grim prospect. But Solomon ends the book by answering the question in Ecclesiastes 11:7–12:14, How can I have joy in the face of aging and death?

Enjoy Life as God Intended
ECCLESIASTES 11:7-10

Yes, if this life is all there is, then death renders every action in this cursed world meaningless. However, Solomon has consistently made the point that the fleeting nature of life should cause us to enjoy life the best we can as God intended because it is a gift from God. Death's ominous reality can also render every action meaningful. That is what Solomon calls us to here.

He says that light is sweet, and it is pleasing to see the sun (11:7). What he means is that life is a good gift. We see this in springtime because the gloominess of winter has passed and the sun is out and it's warm outside, and people start spending more time outside enjoying the sun and having a great time. It is a joy. That is kind of what Solomon is talking about here. Being alive under the sun can be sweet. Again, Ecclesiastes has made both points. Being under the sun can be drudgery, and being under the sun can be joy (Murphy, *Proverbs, Ecclesiastes, Song of Songs*, 214). The point is that you should rejoice in all of your days because they are fleeting—life does not last long. This is illustrated in the way we enjoy spring and take advantage of it because we know it will not last forever—summer and fall and then winter are coming right around the corner. In the same way we should enjoy life while we can because it is fleeting.

The mention of light in verse 7 leads the way for what he says about darkness in verse 8. He says to rejoice in however many years you are able to live because the days of darkness will be many, and then he reminds us again that everything that comes in life is "futile"—*hevel*. I believe the best meaning for *hevel* in this passage is "fleeting." He drives the idea home that life is momentary by explaining that the days of being dead—the days of darkness—far outnumber the days of life under the sun (i.e., being alive) (Garrett, *Proverbs, Ecclesiastes, Song of Songs*, 340). Therefore, live life to the full in the face of the fleeting nature of life and the finality of death. Contemplating death is a means to enjoy life and a means to live wisely. As we have seen in Ecclesiastes, when you contemplate death you are better at avoiding the things that might cause an early death. When you are young, you do not count your days. You think you have countless days ahead, and that can lead you to do something foolish. And when you contemplate death, you are better at enjoying life in the present.

The next verse (11:9) commands us not to postpone enjoyment to some future time. Young people tend to think they will really be able to enjoy life when they grow up. We think when I have a car, when I graduate college, when I get out on my own, or when I start a family, then I can really start living life (Greidanus, *Preaching Christ*, 287). Solomon says, "No! Enjoy the present moment." Country songs like "Don't Blink" and "You're Gonna Miss This" really have a way of helping us not take life for granted. For example, in "Don't Blink," Kenny Chesney sings about seeing an old man in his 100s being interviewed and saying that the secret to life is not blinking because life goes by so fast. Before you know it, you go from grade school to meeting your high school sweetheart to getting married to your babies growing up to your wife's death. So enjoy every moment of your life and live it for all it is worth.

In the song "You're Gonna Miss This," Trace Adkins talks about a mom driving her teenage daughter to school, and the daughter laments the fact that she is under age. The daughter talks about how she can't wait till she becomes an adult and can do what she wants, but her mom tells her to slow down because she will miss the teen years once they are gone. Later on she is a newlywed living in a small apartment, and when her dad visits her, she starts talking about how she can't wait to be a mom and have a house of her own. Her dad tells her to have patience and enjoy these days because she will miss them once they are gone. Down the road, she has a young family with all the chaos that comes with it. A plumber comes to the house, and she keeps apologizing for the noise and the chaos. He says it is not a problem; in fact, there will come a day when her kids are grown that she will miss these days. The song encourages us to slow down and enjoy every day for the gift that it is.

Accordingly, Solomon exhorts his readers to rejoice in their youth and to walk in the ways of their hearts and eyes, but he adds that they must recognize that God will judge in the end (11:9). Enjoy life's prime and the opportunities you have now that others do not have; do what you want to do. Seize the day! However, keep in mind that you will face God and answer for how you lived your life. Ecclesiastes has speculated throughout about a final judgment. The message has been clear that from a human perspective we cannot know for sure what happens beyond death, but Solomon says here that there is something beyond the grave—judgment for how you lived.

Some might see the inevitability of judgment as a drag, but Solomon does not mention judgment here to be a damper. Instead, Solomon references judgment to encourage the reader to enjoy life, but to enjoy life as God intended, not following after our "own thoughts" (Isa 65:2; cf. Eccl 7:29). The book has longed for judgment—for things to be set right. One thing judgment does is make our actions meaningful. God takes us seriously as human beings. What we do matters to Him (Kidner, *Ecclesiastes*, 99). Therefore, enjoy life responsibly as God designed. That means we don't determine for ourselves how we will do marriage, food, drink, sex, finances, family, work, and relationships. We enjoy things in those areas of life the way the Bible has instructed us to. That's how we seize the day.

Lastly, in this section Solomon says to remove "sorrow" and "pain" from your body because youth is fleeting (11:10). The word translated "prime of life" literally means "black hair" as opposed to the gray hair of old age (Garrett, *Proverbs, Ecclesiastes, Song of Songs*, 340). Since youth is fleeting, and your black hair will turn gray (or fall out!) faster than you realize, you must remove sorrow and pain from your life.

There are two things that the person must remove from life to enjoy their fleeting youth properly. First, you must remove *sorrow* to enjoy youth responsibly. Do not idolize the state of youth to the point that you dread its loss and thus fail to enjoy the gift while you have it (Kidner, *Message of Ecclesiastes*, 99).

My friend Chip told me one time about a pair of shoes he got as a boy for Christmas. The shoes would light up every time they hit the pavement. He wore them all Christmas day and loved them, but his mom warned him, "Be careful. Once the battery goes out, they won't light up anymore." He said that he was so worried about running the battery out that he barely ever wore the shoes again, and then his feet got too big. We can waste a great gift if we never use it. We can also waste the gifts of youth. We should see youth as beautiful in its time but passing and not ultimate. Thus, do not let the problems and fleetingness of life spoil your youth. Do not let youth's transitory nature cause you to miss out on enjoying what you have. As Ferris Beuller says, "Life moves pretty fast. If you don't stop and look around once in a while, you could miss it."

Second, the other thing that can spoil your youth and must be removed from your life is *sin*. The HCSB translates the word "pain," but the word is literally "evil." To "put away pain," then, is to repent of sin. God has made life as a gift to be enjoyed as He designed. We run into major problems when we depart from His good design. When we choose to do marriage, relationships, food, money, and work in ways He did not intend, it leads to brokenness and pain in our lives. So when you depart from God's design, repent and turn to Him. . . . That's what Solomon says next.

Turn to God Now before Aging Robs You
ECCLESIASTES 12:1-7

Solomon's intention in this section is to explain that today is the day to turn to God—don't delay. He's exhorted us to enjoy life, and as we have seen, turning to God is the only way to enjoy life rightly. In order to accomplish his purpose, Solomon gives a sobering picture of the curse of death with the hope that it will drive us to God now. Murphy points out that the poem is relentless in its move toward death. This entire section is one long run-on sentence that if read together would literally leave the reader out of breath (Murphy, *Proverbs, Ecclesiastes, Song of Songs*, 215).

Solomon commands us to remember our Creator in the days of our youth (12:1). What does that entail? Remembering your Creator means trusting Him, obeying Him, and walking with Him. It entails teaching your kids about God (Deut 6). The reference to God as Creator here looks back to the creation event, which has been the backdrop to Ecclesiastes all along. Joy can truly be found if one lives

out the wise order by which God created the world. God created everything good and to be enjoyed; however, because we sinned, now everything is broken. We now use things—even good things—wrongly or
worship them as idols, and that departure from God's design leads
to brokenness. Solomon has catalogued this throughout Ecclesiastes
concerning pleasure, comedy, success, wisdom, money, extravagant
possessions, and so much more. The only way to navigate this world
wisely and truly enjoy the good gifts God has created for us—not as
idols we place above Him but as gifts meant to glorify Him—is by faith
in Him, so we are called to repent of our sin, repent of our idolatry,
and believe in Him.

Johnny Hunt points out that you "cannot afford to put off faith in
God" until you are older (*Ecclesiastes*, 73). You will regret it because not
living your life with God at the center causes you to make stupid decisions: you might do something like marry an idiot, choose the wrong
friends, or start the wrong occupation (Chandler, "To the Young and
Old"). Those dumb decisions will have repercussions for the next 30
years of your life or even longer. Tons of money is spent on counsel-
ing and medications because of poor life choices (Driscoll, "Threading
Your Needle"). So turn to God now and submit yourself to His Word for
decision making.

The vocabulary of the poem is apocalyptic. It uses language
often used in passages that describe the end of the world, such as
the darkening of the sun and moon (cf. Joel 3:15). The point in
Ecclesiastes 12 is that your world personally will end in death. In the
poem the author gives three "before" statements to depict vividly
aging and dying. First, we must turn to God before evil days come
(12:1), which refers to impending death. Death is not the way the
world should be. It was not part of God's original design but rather
is an enemy intruder in the world. When those evil days come, we
will have no pleasure in them (12:1). The depressing reality for many
people is that if they live long enough, they will become so sick,
experience so much daily pain, or feel the indignity of not being
able to do everyday things they used to do with no thought, and they
will beg God to let them die. They will ask God why they continue to
live, and they will hope for death.

Second, we must turn to God before the astrological lights go out
(12:2). We need to understand as we walk through the poem that it
contains highly metaphorical language, and we cannot be dogmatic

about what it all means. However, we can make some observations that come close, I think.[7] Solomon says the lights will go out, which may refer to eye failure or the loss of mental powers. The reference to rain and clouds could refer to glaucoma (i.e., cloudy vision) or that our reasoning and memory functions decline in old age—after all, even when young people forget something, they say they had a "senior moment." Perhaps Solomon is alluding to the heartbreaking effects of dementia. Others think the clouds could refer to troubles that were minor setbacks in youth, but now the aged do not recover as quickly from them, or they never recover from them. Thus, the clouds never go away (Kidner, *Ecclesiastes*, 102).

Solomon continues this section by talking about

> *the day when the guardians of the house tremble, and the strong men stoop, the women who grind cease because they are few, and the ones who watch through the windows see dimly, the doors at the street are shut while the sound of the mill fades.* (12:3-4)

These images refer, it seems, to the diminished capacity of the senses and motor skills in old age. In old age your hands tremble (i.e., the guardians), major muscles fail so you begin to bend over (i.e., the strong men), teeth go missing and chewing is difficult (i.e., the grinders), eyesight dims (i.e., the watchers), and hearing fades (i.e., the doors). The cruel irony is that while your hearing fades, the slightest noise—like a bird chirping—startles and wakes you (12:4). In old age sleeping is difficult—you're up with the birds!

He continues by saying that

> *they are afraid of heights and dangers on the road; the almond tree blossoms, the grasshopper loses its spring, and the caper berry has no effect; for man is headed to his eternal home, and mourners will walk around in the street.* (12:5)

The elderly are afraid of heights, and they are also afraid of falling, or danger in the road, that is, being jostled, in contrast to the courage of youth. The blossoming almond tree refers to white hair in old age, and then after the bloom the hair goes away and you are bald. The

---

[7] Much of this section is dependent on Duane Garrett's helpful analysis of these verses. See Garrett, *Proverbs, Ecclesiastes Song of Songs*, 341–43.

burdened grasshopper can refer to something light that is now too heavy to lift with the vigor of youth gone, or it may refer to bad joints and the loss of mobility. Finally, there is a loss of sexual desire. The caper berry was a known aphrodisiac, but now it has no effect. As Matt Chandler humorously points out, Solomon notoriously loved women and managed to put the loss of sexual appetite dead last. He has no teeth, he cannot move, he cannot see, he cannot hear, and *finally* he is not interested in sex anymore ("To the Young and Old"). This description of aging and the nearing of death is similar to the death of King David in 1 Kings 1. He is cold and cannot keep warm, so they put a beautiful young woman in bed with him to try to warm him up, but the Bible says nothing happens. The only thing left is death. Adam goes to his eternal home, which does not refer to heaven in the context of Ecclesiastes. Throughout the book the author has limited his observations to a human perspective, and therefore he is uncertain about what lies beyond the grave since no human can know for certain. The eternal home merely refers to death itself, which is then followed by a funeral with mourners.

Third, we must turn to God "before the silver cord is snapped, and the gold bowl is broken, and the jar is shattered at the spring, and the wheel is broken into the well" (12:6). The images of the silver cord, the golden bowl, the shattered jar, and the broken wheel refer to drawing water. The problem is that the system to get life-sustaining water has deteriorated and shattered into the finality of death (Webb, *Five Festal Garments*, 99). The cord that pulls the water, the bowl that holds the jar, the jar that holds the water, and the wheel for the pulley system are all broken at the bottom of the well. Life has gone out. The outcome is that man returns to dust (12:7), that is, he dies and decays under the curse of sin while the breath of life returns to God. Again, this is not a comment on heaven. It refers to the departure of life. This reality is the sentence God passed on Adam because of his sin and his posterity's sin (Gen 3; Rom 5). When you sin against God, you shall surely die and return to the dust from which you came. Ecclesiastes has said all along that we live in a cursed world where death is inevitable because of humanity's sinful choices that led us to this point.

The text is painful, depressing, and heartrending, but death's sting should stir us to action. Remember God now when you can avoid living with regret. That exhortation leads to the conclusion of Ecclesiastes.

Trust in Jesus as Your Savior and Sage
ECCLESIASTES 12:8-14

Ecclesiastes 12:8 gives the final assessment, which is the same as the first assessment in Ecclesiastes 1:2: everything is futile, fleeting, meaningless, and absurd. The conclusion helps us understand the purpose behind exposing the meaninglessness of life. Solomon wants us to realize that God imposed a curse on the world to show us the meaninglessness of following our own devices and to drive us to Him. Thus, the point of Ecclesiastes, like every book of the Old Testament, is ultimately to make you wise for salvation through faith in Jesus Christ (2 Tim 3:15). When we see death up close in hospital visits, the suffering of a loved one, or the passing of a friend, it signals that there is something better out there. That's the point of Ecclesiastes: everything is meaningless without Jesus. We see this in the conclusion (12:9-14)

Solomon wrote Ecclesiastes to shepherd the reader with words that are pleasing, true, convicting, and wise (12:9-10). His words are like goads, spiked sticks that prod cattle down the right path. That has been his intention all along. He gives messianic wisdom to convict us of the meaninglessness of life without God and to drive us to remember our Creator. After all, the image of the "one Shepherd" is only used in reference to the Messiah (see Ezek 34:23; 37:24).

Solomon turns his attention to his son, pleading with him to beware of moving beyond his words (12:12). He trains his son in wisdom in order to establish the kingdom, so he tells his son not to attempt his own investigation as if the son could find meaning somewhere that Solomon failed to look. Solomon says his words recorded in Ecclesiastes are sufficient. This is the sum total of the matter (v. 13). Solomon knows the temptation to try anything and everything other than God to find satisfaction, so he has talked about his pursuit of wealth, education, women, pleasure, success, and other things. When all is said and done, God is the only One who can satisfy the human heart.

Solomon, therefore, teaches his son not to try his own search for meaning and to take Solomon's words to heart. Here is the bottom line: "Fear God and keep His commands," since that is our chief end in the light of judgment (12:13-14). The book has longed for judgment because of the injustice in the world, but the problem for us is our part in the injustice of the world. God will set all things right, the wicked will not finally prosper, and the righteous will not finally suffer, but the difficulty for us is that Ecclesiastes makes clear we have failed to keep God's commands. Everyone has failed, including Solomon and his son. Within Solomon's lifetime he went from being the wisest man on planet Earth to sanctioning the sacrifice of babies, all because he saw some hot foreign women he wanted to be his. Yes, Solomon was a great sinner, and we might try to assuage our guilt by saying, "But I never had a thousand wives." Still, you are not without guilt. You have your fantasies and your online history. Ecclesiastes ends by saying even the secret things we think are hidden will see the light of day in judgment when we are completely laid bare and exposed before the holy God (v. 14). That's frightening.

We are under condemnation; that's the bad news. But the good news is that there is one who is greater than Solomon who has come on the scene. He is the Wisdom of God. He does not just teach us messianic wisdom and fail to live up to it; He perfectly lives out the wisdom of God. And yet the One who perfectly lived out the wisdom of God took the judgment for our folly on the cross. He experienced everything we should experience for falling short of God's glory. The enemy—the curse of sin and death—will steal our hearing, steal our motor skills, steal our sight, and steal our youthful vigor, but Jesus redeems us by becoming a curse for us (Gal 3:13). He took on our death. He took on three dark days in the grave, unable to hear, unable to walk, and unable to see. But He did not decay into the dust; He walked away from death. As Jaroslav Pelikan says, "If Christ is risen—then nothing else matters. And if Christ is not risen—then nothing else matters." Because of Christ, the decay of death is not the final word. Because of Christ, aging is not the end. Because of Christ, life can be meaningful, and youthful radiance will last in eternal life after the grave.

Life is meaningful because Christ reconciles us to the Creator of life and gives us the ability to be wise. Now, in Christ, we can be satisfied in God alone, rather than loving His gifts more than we love Him. We can now experience true joy, true meaning.

Conclusion

Only when you trust God fully and are satisfied in Him alone can you truly enjoy life. God has a design for everything. We are meant to enjoy such things as food, drink, relationships, sex, work, and money as a means of worshiping Him. The problem is that we depart from God's good design. We turn the gifts into idols. This reality is one of the fundamental issues Ecclesiastes has uncovered for us: we worship the gift rather than the Giver. Doing so is not just wrong—although it is—it is also unsatisfying. It causes brokenness and meaninglessness. Still, we continue to do it because we think the next thing we move on to will bring us the satisfaction we so desire. We do it with money and possessions, we do it with sex (like Hozier's song "Take Me to Church"), we do it with work success, and we do it with pleasure. These things are fleeting joys at best and cannot satisfy, so we end up broken. Here is the good news: Christ took on our brokenness, and if we repent and believe, then we can recover and pursue God's design for our lives and live life as we are meant to live it. Now, fully satisfied in Jesus, you can enjoy money as one who is content and generous, sex with your covenant spouse in marriage, work as one who provides for his family, and much more in the way God intended. All of these things are meaningless without Jesus, but with Jesus you can live a meaningful life here and hereafter.

Reflect and Discuss

1. In what ways do we try to ignore old age and escape aging?
2. What are some reasons you think we prize youth in our culture? Why is that good, and why might it be bad as well?
3. What are some times in our lives when death confronts us? How might those experiences be helpful?
4. Do you find yourself living life looking to some future when you can really be happy? What keeps you from enjoying the present?
5. What are some practical ways you can enjoy life as God intended?
6. What are some practical ways you can remember your Creator in your youth?
7. What are some major decisions we make in our youth that may have long-term negative consequences if we fail to make godly ones?
8. What do the devastating effects of aging tell us about the human condition?
9. Why did the Spirit inspire such a "depressing" book to be written? How is the book of Ecclesiastes actually "good news/gospel"?
10. What are some ways Ecclesiastes points us to Jesus?

The Preacher on Preaching
(Wisdom from a Wise Wordsmith)
ECCLESIASTES 12:9-14

Main Idea: A preacher should teach the people wisdom using wise words that point them to Jesus and call them to fear and obey God.

I.   **Instruction (12:9-10)**
II. **Admonition (12:11-12)**
III. **Exhortation (12:11,13-14)**

When pastors stand to preach the infallible and inerrant Word of God, the glorious gospel of Jesus Christ, and "the faith that was delivered to the saints once for all" (Jude 3), there is an essential and necessary plumb line that must always guide the God-called messenger: *What* you say is more important than how you say it. But *how* you say it has never been more important.

This plumb line, this dictum, this homiletical "must" statement has biblical warrant and support. We find it embedded in the wisdom of Solomon when he says in Ecclesiastes 12:9-10 that the wise Preacher (ESV) or Teacher (HCSB) "taught the people knowledge . . . words of truth" (the *what*) and that he "sought to find delightful sayings ["acceptable words" NKJV; "just the right words" NIV] . . . like goads, and . . . firmly embedded nails" (the *how*). As he draws this book to a close, the Teacher talks about sound instruction that is presented in an attractive and compelling manner. This is how he has sought to present his thoughts in Ecclesiastes. He reminds us it is important to say the right thing and in the right way.

Martin Lloyd-Jones said, "What is preaching? Logic on fire. Eloquent reason! Are these contradictions? Of course they are not!" (*Preaching and Preachers*, 97).

Logic → what   *Fire* → how

Eloquent → how   *Reason* → what

In this final paragraph we find wisdom wrapped in spiritual logic and passion as we consider "the conclusion of the matter," as we think well about what is most important. Here we find solid insight for those with the assignment to teach God's people God's Word.

Instruction
ECCLESIASTES 12:9-10

In this text the Teacher or Preacher, *Qoheleth*, addresses the proper means of teaching truth to God's people. His primary focus here is written words. However, written words of truth will almost always become spoken words of truth. Similar principles are pertinent for effectively delivering either a written or a spoken message.

Solomon begins by saying, "The Teacher being a wise man" had a certain approach or strategy that shaped and guided his teaching. It was "knowledge" (v. 9) and "truth" (v. 10) delivered with acceptable or delightful words that led his students to "fear God and keep His commands" (v. 13). In other words, he faithfully taught his students the Word of God. And he sought to do so in an appealing and attractive manner. God provided the message; he was simply the messenger. This goal for preaching is reflected in Article XXV of the "Chicago Statement on Hermeneutics" penned in 1982. This statement is rooted in a commitment to the Bible as the inerrant and infallible Word of God. It reads,

> **We affirm** that the only type of preaching which sufficiently conveys the divine revelation and its proper application to life is that which faithfully expounds the text of Scripture as the Word of God.
>
> **We deny** that the preacher has any message from God apart from the text of Scripture.

Because he is wise, the faithful preacher will be a faithful expositor, an engaging expositor. Now there are several essential elements necessary for engaging exposition.

The wise preacher will impart "knowledge" to his people. There will be content, what could be described as "theological exposition." Such a preaching agenda is the only reasonable and defensible strategy given the nature of the Bible as divine revelation.

John MacArthur is on target when he says,

> The only logical response to inerrant Scripture . . . is to preach
> it expositionally. By expositionally, I mean preaching in such a
> way that the meaning of the Bible passage is presented entirely
> and exactly as it was intended by God. (*Rediscovering*, 35)

Good preaching always involves teaching just as good teaching will
always have an element of preaching. Without it our preaching is tepid
and timid and our people malnourished!

Walt Kaiser addressed this malady back in 1981 when he wrote,

> It is no secret that Christ's Church is not at all in good health
> in many places of the world. She has been languishing because
> she has been fed . . . "junk food." . . .
>
> The Biblical text is often no more than a slogan or refrain
> in the message. . . .
>
> Biblical exposition has become a lost art in contemporary
> preaching. The most neglected of all biblical sections is the
> Old Testament—over three-fourths of divine revelation! . . .
>
> Motto preaching may please the masses in that it is filled
> with a lot of epigrammatic or [modern] proverbial slogans
> and interesting anecdotes, but it will always be a powerless
> word lacking the authority and validation of Scripture. (Kaiser,
> *Toward*, 7, 19, 37, 191)

Haddon Robinson reminds us,

> When a preacher fails to preach the Scriptures, he abandons
> his authority. He confronts his hearers no longer with a
> word from God but only another word from men. (*Biblical
> Preaching*, 18)

Sidney Greidanus, in his book *The Modern Preacher and the Ancient
Text*, says,

> Biblical preaching is a Bible-shaped word imparted in a Bible-
> like way. In expository preaching the biblical text is neither a
> conventional introduction to a sermon on a largely different
> theme, nor a convenient peg on which to hang a ragbag of
> miscellaneous thoughts, but a master which dictates and
> controls what is said. (10–11)

How the preacher delivers the knowledge of God's Word is critically
important. Three essentials are noted in Ecclesiastes 12:9:

- *He pondered or weighed* carefully what he wrote and said.
- *He sought out or explored*—he dug deep into the knowledge content he would present.
- *He set in order or arranged many proverbs*—he considered how best to deliver wise sayings, wisdom, words of truth. Here the word *proverbs* is broader in meaning than our word in English. It has the idea of wise sayings or teachings that are words of divine revelation.

The faithful communicator of biblical truth will be gripped by the realization that the book lying before him is filled with wisdom, for it is the Word of God. He will tremble at the thought of manipulating it or abusing it. He will carry out his assignment under a divine mandate to honor the text in its context as it was given by the Holy Spirit of God, always pointing to the hero of the Bible, Messiah Jesus.

A faithful teacher and preacher will take to heart the wise admonition of Charles Koller:

> In expounding the Word of God, there is a grave responsibility upon the preacher to convey the truth without distortion. . . . With eternities at stake, the hearer cannot afford to be in error, nor can the spiritual teacher whom he trusts. . . . Every man has a right to his opinion, but no man has a right to be wrong in his facts. . . . The integrity of the pulpit demands accuracy, thoroughness, and a scrupulous regard for text and context. (Koller, *Expository Preaching*, 64–65)

A wise preacher will work hard to find the right words as he feeds the sheep under his protection. He will also deliver it in the best way. The phrase "delightful sayings" in 12:10 means "acceptable" (NKJV) or pleasing words.

In other words, not only is *error* a danger to the truth; *dullness* is a danger to the truth. Beautiful truth ought to be packaged and wrapped in an attractive style. Indeed, it is probably a sin to make the Bible boring! It is certainly a dereliction of the preacher's responsibility and high calling.

Good preaching gives attention to form and content, structure and substance. It neglects neither and sees no need in sacrificing one for the other. John MacArthur well says,

> The proper elements in an expository sermon may be summed up as follows:

1. Preaching is expository in purpose. It explains the text.

2. Preaching is logical in flow. It persuades the mind.

3. Preaching is doctrinal in content. It obligates the will.

4. Preaching is pastoral in concern. It feeds the soul.

5. Preaching is imaginative in pattern. It excites the emotion.

6. Preaching is relevant in application. It touches the life. (*Expository Preaching*, 289)

This captures well many of the emphases in these final verses of Ecclesiastes.

But what about this issue of delivery? Lloyd-Jones provides wisdom and insight at this point:

> Be natural; forget yourself; be absorbed in what you are doing and in the realization of the presence of God, and in the glory and the greatness of the Truth that you are preaching . . . that you forget yourself completely. . . . Self is the greatest enemy of the preacher, more so than in the case of any other man in society. And the only way to deal with self is to be so taken up with, and so enraptured by the glory of what you are doing, that you forget yourself altogether. (*Preaching and Preachers*, 264)

He also says,

> A theology which does not take fire, I maintain, is a defective theology; or at least the man's understanding of it is defective. Preaching is theology coming through a man who is on fire. A true understanding and experience of the Truth must lead to this. I say again that a man who can speak about these things dispassionately has no right whatsoever to be in a pulpit; and should never be allowed to enter one. (Lloyd-Jones, *Preaching and Preachers*, 97)

One of the greatest preachers of the nineteenth century also understood the importance of wedding biblical content to an effective delivery, finding delightful words to convey the truth. The faithful Baptist Charles Spurgeon noted,

> When I have thought of the preaching of certain good men, I have wondered, not that the congregation was so small, but that it was so large. The people who listen to them ought to excel in the virtue of patience, for they have grand opportunities of exercising it. Some sermons and prayers lend a colour of support to the theory of Dr. William Hammond, that the brain is not absolutely essential to life. Brethren, . . . you will, none of you, covet earnestly the least gifts, and the dullest mannerisms, for you can obtain them without the exertion of the will. . . . Labour to discharge your ministry, not with the lifeless method of an automaton, but with the freshness and power which will render your ministry largely effectual for its sacred purposes. (*All-Around Ministry*, 316–17)

Qoheleth, the preacher/teacher, teaches us in verse 10 to communicate that which is upright—"words of truth." I cannot think of a better description of Holy Scripture: words that are upright, straight, words of integrity because they are words of truth. I came across a marvelous statement concerning the Bible several years ago. Its source is unknown to me, but its affirmation is powerful. It is simply titled,

The Bible

This book contains the mind of God, the state of man, the way of salvation, the doom of sinners, and the happiness of believers. Its doctrine is holy, its precepts are binding, its histories are true, and its decisions are immutable. Read it to be wise, believe it to be saved, and practice it to be holy.

It contains light to direct you, food to support you, and comfort to cheer you. It is the traveler's map, the pilgrim's staff, the pilot's compass, the soldier's sword, and the Christian's charter.

Here, heaven is opened, and the gates of hell disclosed. Christ is its grand subject, our good its design, and the glory of God its end. It should fill the memory, rule the heart, and guide the feet.

Read it slowly, frequently, prayerfully. It is a mine of wealth, a paradise of glory, and a river of pleasure. It is given you in life, will be opened at the Judgment, and be remembered forever. It involves the highest responsibility, will reward faithful labor, and condemn all who trifle with its sacred contents.

> 'Tis the Book that has for the Ages,
> Lifted man from sin and shame;
> That great message on its pages,
> Will forever be the same.

Never compare the Bible with other books. Comparisons are dangerous. Books speak from earth; the Bible speaks from heaven. Never think or say that the Bible contains the Word of God or that it becomes the Word of God. It *is* the Word of God.

Supernatural in origin, eternal in duration, inexpressible in value, infinite in scope, divine in authorship, regenerative in power, infallible in authority, universal in interest, personal in application, inspired in totality. Read it through. Write it down. Pray it in. Work it out. Pass it on. It is the Word of God.

J. I. Packer says,

> The true idea of preaching is that the preacher should become a mouthpiece for his text, opening it up and applying it as a word from God to his hearers, . . . in order that the text may speak . . . and be heard making each point from his text in such a manner "that [his audience] may discern [the voice of God]." (*God Has Spoken*, 28)

Admonition
ECCLESIASTES 12:11-12

Solomon says in 12:11-12, "The sayings of the wise are like goads" that prick and "nails" that stick. They prick us and help push us in the right direction. They will move us into action—action that leads to us being conformed to the image of Christ (Rom 8:29). Koller says,

> The supreme test of all preaching is: what happens in the pew? To John the Baptist there was accorded the highest tribute that could ever come to a minister of the gospel; when they had heard John, "they followed Jesus!" (*Expository Preaching*, 19)

Wise words are like goads. They prod the sluggish and hesitant into action. They have a power to provide a mental and spiritual stimulus, a spiritual shot in the arm.

These collected saying are like well-driven nails. They stabilize on the one hand and on the other give us something to hang things on. H. C. Leupold says, "They furnish a kind of mental anchorage" (*Ecclesiastes*, 295).

The end of verse 11 is a direct declaration of divine inspiration. The "knowledge" of verse 9 and the "words of truth" of verse 10 are given by one Shepherd, the Lord who is my Shepherd (Ps 23), the good shepherd, Jesus Christ (John 10). The Christological signal is too obvious to ignore or neglect.

J. Stafford Wright warns the preacher, "It is possible to be a miser in accumulating knowledge instead of using it for the benefit of others" ("Ecclesiastes," 1,196). Solomon the realist knows there is no end to book making. Just imagine if he were alive today! And yet he is not down on books, study, or knowledge in principle. He is down on it as an end in itself. Knowledge is not the same as wisdom. It is possible to be smart but not intelligent. It is possible to know a lot but not be wise. God's design for our lives is not to make us smart sinners but godly saints!

If we are not careful and wise, we can linger too long at the "Vanity Fair of Knowledge" only to miss out on the wisdom of God and on a life that is really worth living. This is another lesson for those who live life "under the sun."

Some of us have stayed too long at various Vanity Fairs in life (knowledge, power, sex, popularity, wealth). We have played the fool and given our lives to the wrong things. There is a better way. Let God's Word guide your priorities. Let God's Word chart the course of your life. "Fear God and keep His commandments." That is where Solomon is taking us as he ends his book.

Exhortation
ECCLESIASTES 12:11,13-14

John Piper reminds us,

> It is not the job of the Christian preacher to give people moral
> or psychological pep talks about how to get along in the world;
> someone else can do that . . . most of our people have no one

in the world to tell them, week in and week out, about the supreme beauty and majesty of God. (*Supremacy of God*, 12)

And just where is this "supreme beauty and majesty of God" found? It is found in the glory of Jesus Christ, the "one Shepherd," who is the very face of God. When I preach, I always ask five questions of each and every text:

1. What does this text teach us about *God*?
2. What does this text teach us about *fallen man*?
3. What do I want my people to *know*?
4. What do I want my people to *do*?
5. How does this text *point to Jesus*?

You see, Jesus teaches us in Luke 24 that all of Scripture is about Him—all of it. That includes the book of Ecclesiastes, as we have seen in our verse-by-verse study. We dare not treat the Old Testament, for example, the way a Jewish rabbi would. In this regard Jon and I have been greatly blessed by men like Vos, Ferguson, Greidanus, Goldsworthy, and Keller. To gain just a taste of what Christocentric hermeneutics and homiletics can and should do, listen to the insight of Tim Keller as he scans the redemptive storyline of the Old Testament. He shows us well how the whole Bible points to Messiah Jesus.

It's All About Jesus

- Jesus is the true and better *Adam* who passed the test in the wilderness, not the garden, and whose obedience is imputed to us.
- Jesus is the true and better *Abel* who, though innocently slain by wicked hands, has blood now that cries out, not for our condemnation, but for our acquittal.
- Jesus is the better *Ark of Noah* who carries us safely through the wrath of God revealed from heaven and delivers us to a new earth.
- Jesus is the true and better *Abraham* who answered the call of God to leave all that is comfortable and familiar and go out into the world, not knowing where he went, to create a new people of God.
- Jesus is the true and better *Isaac* who was not just offered up by his father on the mount but was truly sacrificed for us. And

when God said to Abraham, "Now I know you love Me because you did not withhold your son, your only son, whom you love, from Me," now we can look at God taking His Son up the mountain of Calvary and sacrificing Him and say, "Now we know that You love us because You did not withhold Your Son, Your only Son, whom You love, from us."

- Jesus is the true and better *Jacob* who wrestled and took the blow of justice we deserved, so we, like Jacob, only receive the wounds of grace to wake us up and discipline us.

- Jesus is the true and better *Joseph* who, at the right hand of the King, forgives those who betrayed Him and sold Him, and uses His new power to save them.

- Jesus is the true and better *Moses* who stands in the gap between the people and the Lord and who mediates a new covenant.

- Jesus is the true and better *Rock of Moses* who, struck with the rod of God's justice, now gives us living water in the desert.

- Jesus is the true and better *Joshua* who leads us into a land of eternal rest and heavenly blessing.

- Jesus is the better *Ark of the Covenant* who topples and disarms the idols of this world, going Himself into enemy territory, and making an open spectacle of them all.

- Jesus is the true and better *Job*, the truly innocent sufferer, who then intercedes for and saves His stupid friends.

- Jesus is the true and better *David* whose victory becomes His people's victory, though they never lifted a stone to accomplish it themselves.

- Jesus is the true and better *Esther* who didn't just risk leaving an earthly palace but lost the ultimate and heavenly one, who didn't just risk His life, but gave His life to save His people.

- Jesus is the true and better *Daniel*, having been lowered into a lions' den of death and emerging early the next morning alive and vindicated by His God.

- Jesus is the true and better *Jonah* who was cast out into the storm so that we safely could be brought in.

- Jesus is the *real Passover Lamb*, innocent, perfect, helpless, slain, so the angel of death will pass over us.

- He's the *true temple*, the *true prophet*, the *true priest*, the *true king*, the *true sacrifice*, the *true lamb*, the *true light*, and the *true bread*.

- The Bible really is not about you is it? It really is all about Him. (Keller, "It's All about Jesus")

Oh, how this needs to be reflected in our preaching! We must always and continually point people to the "one Shepherd."

The phrase "when all has been heard" (v. 13) could be paraphrased for our day, "When everything is said and done." In other words, What is the bottom line, the endgame? Solomon says it is twofold: (1) fear God and (2) keep His commands. Trust Him and then obey Him. The order is crucial.

"Fear God" means to put God in His proper place, us in our proper place, and all fears, hopes, dreams, and agendas in their proper place. The clear and consistent teaching and encouragement of the Word of God is essential if this is to take place. "Fear God": What does the text teach me about God? "Keep His commandments": What does this teach me about me? "Fear God and keep His commandments": Obey Him out of love and respect for *who* He is and *what* He has done. You see the order, don't you? I am accepted; therefore, I obey! It is not, I obey so that I can be accepted. He loved me first! I now love and serve Him in grateful response.

"Because this is for all humanity" concludes verse 13. The ESV says, "For this is the whole duty of man." Augustine (AD 354–430) said it well: "Thou hast made us for thyself, and our heart is restless till it rest in thee." We will never find rest until we come to rest in Jesus. We will never find rest until we fear Him and obey Him. This is what we were made for.

Verse 14 concludes "the words of the Teacher." They are pointed and they are spiritually ominous. "God will bring every act to judgment, including every hidden thing, whether good or evil." Solomon tells us a day of reckoning is coming. It will be comprehensive and detailed in scope. Every thought and every action will be exposed to the search-light of God's judgment. Not one thing will escape. Not one person will escape.

- "Every act": our actions.
- "Every hidden thing": our thoughts.
- "Good or evil": it will all come to light.

On that day your righteousness will be exposed as filthy, dirty rags. Only the one clothed in the righteousness of Christ will be able to stand before holy God in full acceptance and approval. Will that be you?

Conclusion

One of my spiritual heroes and friends in his last years was the great expositor Stephen Olford (1918–2004). On the wall of his private study hangs a plaque containing a quote from one of Dr. Olford's heroes, Robert Murray M'Cheyne. On that plaque are the words, "Lord, make me as holy as a saved sinner can be!" (Bonar, *Memoir and Remains*, 159).

This is a good word from a great preacher. This is a good word for any follower of Jesus. This is a good word for any preacher who understands the exhortation of *Qoheleth*, "Fear God and keep his commandments, for this is the whole duty of man" (NIV).

Cotton Mather, the American Puritan, accurately assessed the nature of the holy assignment of the preacher when he said,

> The office of the Christian ministry, rightly understood, is the honorable and most important, that any man in the whole world can ever sustain; and it will be one of the wonders and employments of eternity to consider the reasons why the wisdom and goodness of God assigned this office to imperfect and guilty man! (Quoted in Stott, *Between Two Worlds*, 31)

The preacher has given us wise words on preaching. We need to hear his counsel. We need to act on his instruction. Let's preach and teach beautiful truth in a beautiful way all for the glory of a beautiful Savior whose name is Jesus. Too much is at stake for us to do anything less.

Reflect and Discuss

1. Why does an infallible and inerrant Bible demand faithful preaching?
2. Do you think how we teach the Bible is really important? Why or why not?
3. What are your thoughts on Article XXV of the Chicago Statement?
4. John MacArthur says expositional preaching is the only logical response to an inerrant Bible. Do you agree or disagree? Why?
5. Lloyd-Jones calls real preaching "logic on fire." What does he mean by this?
6. MacArthur notes six components of proper expository preaching. Discuss them.

7. Packer says preachers should be "a mouthpiece for the text." What do you think?

8. We ask five questions of every text. Walk through them and discuss them.

9. Discuss Keller's "It's All About Jesus." Do you agree with his approach?

10. How has Ecclesiastes pointed us to Jesus in these 12 chapters?

WORKS CITED

Begg, Alistair. "All Those Lonely People." Sermon preached at Parkside Church, Chagrin Falls, OH, November 2, 2002. https://www.truthforlife.org/resources/sermon/all-those-lonely-people.

———. "Concerning Worship." Sermon preached at Parkside Church, Chagrin Falls, OH, November 17, 2002. https://www.truthforlife.org/resources/sermon/concerning-worship.

———. "Eternity on My Mind." Sermon preached at Parkside Church, Chagrin Falls, OH, January 15, 2010. https://www.truthforlife.org/resources/sermon/eternity-my-mind.

———. "In Search of Meaning." Sermon preached at Parkside Church, Chagrin Falls, OH, November 24, 2002. https://www.truthforlife.org/resources/sermon/in-search-of-meaning.

———. "The Search for Satisfaction." Sermon preached at Parkside Church, Chagrin Falls, OH, October 27, 2002. https://www.truthforlife.org/resources/sermon/the-search-for-satisfaction.

———. "A Word to the Wise." Sermon preached at Parkside Church, Chagrin Falls, OH, December 3, 2009. https://www.truthforlife.org/resources/sermon/a-word-to-the-wise.

Blair, Leonardo. "Victoria Osteen Ripped for Telling Church 'Just Do Good for Your Own Self'; Worship Is Not for God, 'You're Doing It for Yourself.'" *The Christian Post*, August 30, 2014. Accessed November 2, 2015. http://www.christianpost.com/news/victoria-osteen-ripped-for-telling-church-just-do-good-for-your-own-self-worship-is-not-for-god-youre-doing-it-for-yourself-125636.

Bonar, Andrew. *Memoir and Remains of Robert Murray M'Cheyne.* Carlisle, PA: Banner of Truth Trust, 2004.

Brennan, John. "Athletes and Going for 'Broke.'" *Meadowlands Matters* (blog). *NorthJersey.com.* October 3, 2012. http://blog.northjersey.com/meadowlandsmatters/3700/athletes-and-going-for-%E2%80%9Cbroke%E2%80%9D.

Buchanan, Kyle. "Leading Men Age, but Their Love Interests Don't." *Browbeat* (blog). *Slate.* May 26, 2015. http://www.slate.com/blogs /browbeat/2015/05/26/leading_men_age_but_their_love_interest _don_t.html.

Chandler, Matt. "Approaching the Divine." Sermon preached at The Village Church, Flower Mound, TX, September 3, 2006. http://www.thevillagechurch.net/resources/sermons/detail /approaching-the-divine.

———. "Daily Contact." Sermon preached at The Village Church, Flower Mound, TX, December 3, 2006. http://www.thevillagechurch .net/resources/sermons/detail/daily-contact.

———. "The Gift." Sermon preached at The Village Church, Flower Mound, TX, July 30, 2006. http://www.thevillagechurch.net /resources/sermons/detail/the-gift.

———. "Ingredients." Sermon preached at The Village Church, Flower Mound, TX, August 6, 2006. http://www.thevillagechurch.net /resources/sermons/detail/ingredients.

———. "Out of Breath." Sermon preached at The Village Church, Flower Mound, TX, August 20, 2006. http://www.thevillagechurch.net /resources/sermons/detail/out-of-breath.

———. "Quenched." Sermon preached at The Village Church, Flower Mound, TX, July 16, 2006. http://www.thevillagechurch.net /resources/sermons/detail/quenched.

———. "The Sixth Sense." Sermon preached at The Village Church, Flower Mound, TX, July 9, 2006. http://www.thevillagechurch.net /resources/sermons/detail/the-sixth-sense.

———. "To the Young and Old." Sermon preached at The Village Church, Flower Mound, TX, December 17, 2006. http://www.thevillage church.net/resources/sermons/detail/to-the-young-and-the-old.

Criswell, W. A. "The Pattern of Pessimism." Sermon preached at First Baptist Church of Dallas. Dallas, TX, December 29, 1991. http:// www.wacriswell.com/sermons/1991/the-pattern-of-pessimism.

Dever, Mark. "The Ungodly." Sermon preached at Capitol Hill Baptist Church, Washington, D.C., May 16, 1999. http://resources .thegospelcoalition.org/library/the-ungodly.

Driscoll, Mark. "Cleaning Your Plate." Sermon preached at Mars Hill Church, Seattle WA, June 29, 2003. http://legacy.thegospelcoalition .org/resources/entry/Cleaning-Your-Plate.

————. "The Gift of Death." Sermon preached at Mars Hill Church, Seattle WA, April 13, 2003. http://legacy.thegospelcoalition.org /resources/entry/The-Gift-of-Death.

————. "A Goose Chase without a Goose." Sermon preached at Mars Hill Church, Seattle WA, March 23, 2003. http://legacy.thegospel coalition.org/resources/entry/A-Goose-Chase-Without-a-Goose.

————. "Guarding Your Steps." Sermon preached at Mars Hill Church, Seattle WA, May 4, 2003. http://legacy.thegospelcoalition.org /resources/entry/Guarding-Your-Steps.

————. "Peering Over the Loom." Sermon preached at Mars Hill Church, Seattle WA, April 6, 2003. http://legacy.thegospelcoalition .org/resources/entry/Peering-Over-the-Loom.

————. "Redefining Riches." Sermon preached at Mars Hill Church, Seattle WA, May 25, 2003. http://legacy.thegospelcoalition.org /resources/entry/Redefining-Riches.

————. "Setting the Record Crooked." Sermon preached at Mars Hill Church, Seattle WA, March 16, 2003. http://legacy.thegospel coalition.org/resources/entry/Setting-the-Record-Crooked.

————. "Threading Your Needle." Sermon preached at Mars Hill Church, Seattle WA, July 27, 2003. http://legacy.thegospelcoalition .org/resources/scripture-index/ecclesiastes/author/mark_driscoll.

Elshof, Greg. *I Told Me So: Self-Deception and the Christian Life*. Grand Rapids: Eerdmans, 2009.

Enns, Peter. *Ecclesiastes*. Two Horizons Old Testament Commentary. Grand Rapids: Eerdmans, 2011.

Eswine, Zack. *Recovering Eden: The Gospel According to Ecclesiastes*. Phillipsburg, NJ: P&R, 2014.

Ferguson, Sinclair. *The Pundit's Folly: Chronicles of an Empty Life*. Edinburgh: Banner of Truth Trust, 1995.

Garrett, Duane. *Proverbs, Ecclesiastes, Song of Songs*. NAC 14. Nashville: B&H, 1993.

Greidanus, Sidney. *The Modern Preacher and the Ancient Text: Interpreting and Preaching Biblical Literature*. Grand Rapids: Eerdmans, 1988.

————. *Preaching Christ from Ecclesiastes*. Grand Rapids: Eerdmans, 2010.

Hamilton, James M. *God's Glory in Salvation through Judgment*. Wheaton, IL: Crossway, 2010.

Hunt, Johnny. *The Book of Ecclesiastes: An Archive of Exegetical Sermon Notes*. Woodstock: 3H, 2008.

Kaiser Walter C., Jr. *Toward an Exegetical Theology: Biblical Exegesis for Preaching and Teaching.* Grand Rapids: Baker, 1981.
Keller, Tim. "It's All about Jesus." *Theology and Quotations* (blog). December 4, 2006. http://www.danielakin.com/wp-content /uploads/2012/02/Matthew-5.17-18-What-Did-Jesus-Believe -About-the-Bible-20.20-Manuscript.pdf. Slightly revised.
———. "Problem of History: Does the Harshness of Life Make Sense?" Sermon preached at Redeemer Presbyterian Church, New York City, July 14, 1992. http://www.gospelinlife.com/sermons/problem -of-history-does-the-harshness-of-life-make-sense.
———. "Problem of Meaning: Is There Any Reason for Existence?" Sermon preached at Redeemer Presbyterian Church, New York City, May 31, 1992. http://www.gospelinlife.com/sermons/problem -of-meaning-is-there-any-reason-for-existence.html.
———. "The Search for Achievement." Sermon preached at Redeemer Presbyterian Church, New York City, September 27, 1998. http:// www.gospelinlife.com/sermons/the-search-for-achievement.
———. "The Search for Justice." Sermon preached at Redeemer Presbyterian Church, New York City, September 13, 1998. http:// www.gospelinlife.com/sermons/the-search-for-justice.
———. "The Search for Pleasure." Sermon preached at Redeemer Presbyterian Church, New York City, September 20, 1998. http:// www.gospelinlife.com/sermons/the-search-for-pleasure.
Kidner, Derek. *The Message of Ecclesiastes: A Time to Mourn, and a Time to Dance.* Downers Grove, IL: IVP, 1976.
Koller, Charles. *Expository Preaching Without Notes.* Grand Rapids: Baker, 1962.
Lavery, David. *Seinfeld, Master of Its Domain: Revisiting Television's Greatest Sitcom.* New York: Bloomsbury, 2006.
Leupold, H. C. *Exposition of Ecclesiastes.* Grand Rapids: Baker, 1952.
Lewis, Michael. "What Wealth Does to Your Soul." *The Week.* January 2, 2015. http://theweek.com/articles/441315/what-wealth-does-soul.
Lloyd-Jones, D. Martyn. *Preaching and Preachers.* Grand Rapids: Zondervan, 1971.
Longman, Tremper, III. *The Book of Ecclesiastes.* NICOT. Grand Rapids: Eerdmans, 1998.
MacArthur, John. *Rediscovering Expository Preaching: Balancing the Art and Science of Biblical Exposition.* Dallas: Word, 1992.

Moore, Russell. "Let Us Eat." Twitter. April 5, 2015. https://twitter.com /drmoore/status/584699323444789248.

Murphy, Roland, and Elizabeth Huwiler. *Proverbs, Ecclesiastes, Song of Songs*. New International Biblical Commentary. Peabody, MA: Hendrickson, 1999.

O'Donnell, Douglas Sean. *Ecclesiastes*. Reformed Expository Commentary. Phillipsburg, NJ: P&R, 2014.

Packer, J. I. *God Has Spoken*. Downers Grove: IVP, 1979.

Perrin, Nicholas. "Messianism in the Narrative Frame of Ecclesiastes." *RB* 108 (2001): 51–57.

Piper, John. *The Supremacy of God in Preaching*. Grand Rapids: Baker, 1993.

Provan, Iaia. *Proverbs, Ecclesiastes*. New International Version Application Commentary. Grand Rapids: Zondervan, 2001.

Roberts, Chris. "My Journey to Atheism: Faithful Christian Living." *The Book of Wonder* (blog). September 5, 2014. https://www.thebookof wonder.org/2014/09/journey-atheism-faithful-christian-living.

Robinson, Haddon. *Biblical Preaching: The Development and Delivery of Expository Messages*. Grand Rapids: Baker, 1980.

Russell, Bertrand. *The Autobiography of Bertrand Russell*. New York: Routledge, 2000.

Scraton, Phil. *Hillsborough: The Truth*. Edinburgh: Mainstream, 2009.

Scroggins, Jimmy. "3 Circles—Life Conversation Guide." *North American Mission Board*. Vimeo. May 22, 2014. https://vimeo.com/96082854.

Shilito, Edward. "Jesus of the Scars." 1919. Reprint. *The Jesus Question* (blog). October 28, 2013. http://thejesusquestion.org /2013/10/28/jesus-of-the-scars-by-edward-shillito.

Sjogren, Bob. "Cat and Dog Theology." *Unveiling Glory*. http://www .unveilinglory.com/content/view/59/80.

Spurgeon, C. H. *An All-Around Ministry*. Edinburgh: Banner of Truth Trust, 1960.

Stott, John. *Between Two Worlds*. Grand Rapids: Eerdmans, 1982.

Sullivan, Laura. "In Search of the Red Cross' $500 Million in Haiti Relief." Special Report: The American Red Cross. NPR. June 3, 2015. http://www.npr.org/2015/06/03/411524156/in-search-of-the-red -cross-500-million-in-haiti-relief?utm_source=twitter.com&utm _medium=social&utm_campaign=npr&utm_term=nprnews&utm _content=20150603.

Swindoll, Charles R. *Living on the Ragged Edge: Finding Joy in a World Gone Mad.* Nashville: Thomas Nelson, 2005.

Torre, Pablo S. "How (and Why) Athletes Go Broke." *The Vault* (blog). *Sports Illustrated.* March 23, 2009. http://www.si.com/vault/2009/03/23/105789480/how-and-why-athletes-go-broke.

Voorhees, Tim. "Why Most Families Lose Their Wealth by the Third Generation." Accessed November 3, 2015. https://www.wealthcounsel.com/articles/2009/why-most-families-lose-their-wealth-by-the-third-generation.

Webb, Barry. *Five Festal Garments.* New Studies in Biblical Theology. Downers Grove: IVP, 2000.

Wikipedia. "Turn! Turn! Turn!" https://en.wikipedia.org/wiki/Turn!_Turn!_Turn!

Wright, J. Stafford. "Ecclesiastes." Pages 1137–97 in volume 5 of *The Expositor's Bible Commentary.* Grand Rapids: Zondervan, 1986.

SCRIPTURE INDEX